Fifty Famous Australians

Nancy Wake parachuted into enemy territory while working for the French Resistance during World War II.

Weary Dunlop stood in front of an injured man to stop him being bayoneted to death.

Nicole Kidman dressed up in a woolly car seat cover to play a sheep in the Nativity Play at school.

But what could **Charles Kingsford Smith** do while standing on his head?

The triumphs, the tears, the tantrums and the tantalising facts about fifty famous Australians are all here in one bumper volume. From Ned Kelly to Kylie Minogue, their personal stories and achievements have helped shape the face of Australia – in one way or another!

50 famous australians

Meredith Costain

Puffin Books

Puffin Books

Published by the Penguin Group
Penguin Books Australia
250 Camberwell Road
Camberwell, Victoria 3124, Australia
Penguin Books Ltd
80 Strand, London WC2R ORL, England
Penguin Putnam Inc.
375 Hudson Street, New York, New York 10014, USA
Penguin Books, a division of Pearson Canada
10 Alcorn Avenue, Toronto, Ontario, Canada, M4V 3B2
Penguin Books (N.Z.) Ltd
Cnr Rosedale and Airborne Roads, Albany, Auckland, New Zealand
Penguin Books (South Africa) (Pty) Ltd
24 Sturdee Avenue, Rosebank, Johannesburg 2196, South Africa
Penguin Books India (P) Ltd
11, Community Centre, Panchsheel Park, New Delhi, 110 017, India

First published by Penguin Books Australia, 2003

1 3 5 7 9 10 8 6 4 2

Cover and text design by Debra Billson, Penguin Design Studio
Illustrations by Bob Shields
Typeset in 11.5/17.5 pt Sabon by Post Pre-press Group, Brisbane, Queensland
Printed and bound in Australia by McPherson's Printing Group, Maryborough, Victoria

The photographs in the book are used by permission and courtesy of the following:
Age archives/Courtesy of the *Age*: 46; Mike Bowers/Courtesy of the *Age*: 239; Eddie Jim/Courtesy of
the *Age*: 150; Jim McEwan/Courtesy of the *Age*: 140; Michelle Mossop/Courtesy of the *Age*: 95;
Simon O'Dwyer/Courtesy of the *Age*: 1; Adam Pretty/Courtesy of the *Age*: 16; Viki Yemettas/Courtesy
of the *Age*: 209 Coo-ee Historical Picture Library: 11, 21, 26, 36, 41, 51, 56, 61, 66, 115, 125, 145,
155, 160, 165, 185, 204, 219; Coo-ee Picture Library: 195; Getty Images/Clive Brunskill: 76; Getty
Images/Stuart Hannagan: 214; Getty Images/Anthony Harvey: 170; Getty Images/Warren Little: 234;
Peter Mack: 105; Brett Hartwig/Newspix: 190; John Hawryluk/Newspix: 31; David
Kapernick/Newspix: 229; Peter Kurnik/Newspix: 130; News Ltd/Newspix: 6, 71, 81, 90, 100, 110,
120, 135, 180, 224, 244; Anthony Weate/Newspix: 200.

National Library of Australia
Cataloguing-in-Publication data:

Costain, Meredith, 1955– .
50 famous Australians.

ISBN 0 14 330079 2.

1. Australia – Biography. I. Title.

994.0922

www.puffin.com.au

Contents

Robyn Archer

A singer, writer and director who has performed throughout Australia and the world

Born: 18 June 1948 in Adelaide, South Australia

Personal motto: If you want something, go for it!

Website: www.robynarcher.com.au

Musical beginnings

Robyn Archer was born into a family of entertainers. Her dad was a musician and comedian and her mum played piano and sang. Both her great-grandparents had been music hall entertainers in the East End of London. They all lived together in a pub in northern Adelaide. Every afternoon at five o'clock, Robyn and her great-grandmother high-kicked their way down the stairs to the Ladies Bar. Standing on a table in the middle of the room, Robyn sang naughty songs for the customers. She was only four years old.

Stuck in bed

When she was little, Robyn was so sick with asthma her parents decided not to have any more kids, so they could look after her properly. They told her, 'all you have to do is stay alive and anything else you want to do is okay.' Robyn wasn't able to play much sport, or do normal things like go to sleepovers with her friends. She spent lots of her time stuck in bed, drawing pictures or writing stories, living in the world of her imagination.

A natural performer

Over the years, Robyn's parents continued to give her lots of attention. To build up her lungs, her father took her swimming and encouraged her to sing. Robyn taught herself to play the ukulele, and sang Elvis songs to her primary-school friends. By the time she was twelve she was playing guitar and singing in vaudeville concerts. Four years later she was in cafes playing folk music and singing protest songs against the Vietnam War. She also appeared on several TV variety shows.

The turning point

In the mid-1970s, Robyn was invited to sing with an opera company. It changed her life. She became interested in cabaret: shows featuring songs that, as well as being entertaining, had a message for the audience. Soon she was writing and directing her own cabaret shows, like *The Pack of Women* and *A Star is Torn,* which asked questions about the way women are viewed in society. The shows became sell-out successes, and Robyn toured Australia and overseas. Finally she had found a way to combine her two great passions – performing and teaching.

A woman of many talents

Many of the songs Robyn has written over the years for her cabaret shows have been recorded. She has also written songs for children, including 'Mrs Bottle's

Absolutely Blurtingly Beautiful World-Beating Burp'. These days, Robyn shares her vast experience and knowledge by giving advice to lots of arts boards and councils and organising arts festivals.

Six interesting things about Robyn Archer

1 She can yodel.
2 She has the lung capacity of a seven-year-old child.
3 She was kicked out of her school choir because she sang off-key.
4 She once sang in a show called *I Love You, Humphrey B Bear*.
5 She has written 20 theatre shows, composed over 100 songs and recorded 10 albums.
6 She is the official ambassador of the Adelaide Crows.

Career highlights

1960:	first professional performance at Uraidla RSL Hall, aged twelve
1964–1965:	appearances on the TV show, 'Brian Henderson's Bandstand'

1978:   writes her first cabaret show, *Kold Komfort Kaffee*

1979:   writes the successful show, *A Star is Torn*

1986:   ARIA Award for Best Soundtrack – *The Pack of Women*

1988, 2000: Artistic Director, Adelaide Festival of the Arts

2000:   awarded Officer of the Order of Australia (AO)

2001:   Creator, Tasmanian Festival of the Arts

2002:   awarded a French honour – Chevalier de l'Ordre des Arts et des Lettres

2002, 2003: Artistic Director, Melbourne Festival of the Arts

☞ Guess what?

Although Robyn Archer is one of Australia's most accomplished performers, she has never received any formal training in singing or acting and cannot read music.

Ron Barassi

One of the great legends of Australian
Rules Football

Full name: Ronald Dale Barassi

Born: 27 February 1936 in Castlemaine, Victoria

Position: ruck-rover

A legend is born

Ron Barassi was born in Castlemaine, but spent his early years in Melbourne while his father played football for the Melbourne Football Club. In 1941, the year after Melbourne won the premiership, Ron's dad was killed while fighting in World War II. Five-year-old Ron was sent back to the country to live with his grandad and aunty.

My dad – the hero

Everyone thought that Ron's father had been a hero. Ron was determined to grow up to play football, just like his dad. Except he didn't want to be just any old kind of footballer – he wanted to be the *best*. There weren't any kids living near his grandad's farm, so he kicked the football his mother had sent him to himself. He was fiercely competitive at school, and soon became the best sprinter, long jumper and high jumper in the district.

Like father, like son

Ron moved back to Melbourne when he was eleven. A few years later he began playing football with the Preston Scouts. Footballing friends of his father thought he was good enough to start training with his dad's old team. He was invited to join the Melbourne

football • coaching • media

thirds in 1951. Two years later, aged seventeen, he played his first game for the Melbourne seniors. By 1957 he had two Best Player awards under his belt.

☞ **Guess what?**

Ron Barassi was too small and slight to be a ruckman and too big to be a rover. So a new position was invented for him – ruck-rover. It allowed him to roam all over the ground and stay in the play all the time, kicking and marking. The new position changed the way football was played.

His brilliant career

Over a stunning forty-year career, Ron Barassi has either played with or against, or coached most of football's greatest players. After playing over 200 games for Melbourne, he joined Carlton as captain/coach in 1965, taking them to two premierships in 1968 and 1970. In 1973, he was appointed coach of North Melbourne. His brilliant tactics saw them take out their first Premiership in 1975, then win again in 1977. He coached Melbourne from 1981 to 1985, then after a short retirement returned to the game to coach the

Sydney Swans for three seasons. These days he works as a sports commentator and motivational speaker. In Ron's mind, there is no such word as defeat.

Six interesting things about Ron Barassi

1 When he was a kid he was so lonely he used to talk to a stone he called Rockfist Rogan.

2 He has a terrible memory.

3 He was never afraid to tell umpires exactly what he thought of them.

4 He has played 253 games of football, and coached more than 500 games.

5 He has been involved in 17 Grand Finals, resulting in 10 Premierships.

6 His jumper number is 31, the same number his father wore when he played for Melbourne.

Comeback fever

The 1970 Grand Final between Carlton and Collingwood was the most important game in Barassi's career. It's also become the stuff of legend. At half-time the Carlton Blues were trailing by 44 points. Barassi asked his players to change their moves and tactics. He got them playing a running game where they handballed to each other to get the ball down the field. He also put on a new player – Ted Hopkins – who kicked two goals in the first four minutes, then another two. The Carlton players went handball crazy, playing 'keepings-off'. The Magpies were confused. Carlton won the game by 11 points.

Career highlights

1951:	invited to train with the Melbourne Football Club thirds
1953:	plays first senior game for Melbourne Football Club
1956–57:	awarded Best Player in Grand Final
1965:	joins Carlton as captain/coach
1970:	coaches Carlton to win Grand Final in the greatest comeback in finals history
1973:	appointed coach of North Melbourne
1975:	coaches North Melbourne to their first Premiership
1993:	appointed coach of Sydney Swans

Don Bradman

The world's greatest batsman

Full name: Sir Donald George Bradman

Also known as: The Boy from Bowral, Our Don

Born: 27 August 1908 in Cootamundra,
New South Wales

Died: 25 February 2001 in Kensington,
South Australia

Website: www.donbradman.com.au

Early years

Don Bradman was born in Cootamundra, a country town in New South Wales, and moved to Bowral when he was three. Don loved playing sport when he was a kid, but there weren't any kids of his age around to play with. So he invented his own ball game. He'd throw a golf ball at the round brick base of a water tank, then hit it with a cricket stump as it bounced back towards him. Or he'd catch the ball after aiming it at the bottom railing of a wooden fence. It helped to develop his famous batsman's 'eye' for later life.

Don's big break

Don played his first cricket match when he was eleven, scoring 55 runs. The oval he played on is now known as the 'Bradman Oval'. His amazing batting form soon caught the eye of selectors and he moved to Sydney when he was eighteen to play for St George. By 1927, he was playing Sheffield Shield for New South Wales. His big break came the next year when he was picked to play in the 1928–30 series against England. There was no looking back!

Dirty tricks

By the 1930s, Don was a superstar. He'd broken every batting record around. When the English Test team toured Australia in 1932, they decided to use some dirty tricks to even the score. Their captain, Douglas Jardine, directed his fast bowlers to bowl fast, rising balls at the batsman's body. It made the ball much harder to hit without being caught out by the fieldsmen. The new tactic kept Don's batting average down, and England won the series. After major outrage from the cricket world, bodylining, as the tactic was called, was banned.

A surprise ending

In 1948, Don took the Australian team to England for his last Test. As he walked out onto the field to bat, the crowd cheered loudly. Don faced the first ball confidently, knowing he only needed to hit four runs to round off his Test batting average of 99.94 at a solid 100. Then the unbelievable happened. On the next ball, Don was bowled out for a duck.

Some commentators said he was so moved by the applause from the crowd that his eyes blurred with tears, causing him to miss the ball. Whatever the reason, it was the end of a brilliant career.

After retiring from the game, Don went into business, became a selector, and wrote several books about cricket. He died of pneumonia in 2001 at the age of ninety-two.

Guess what?

When Don's team was playing in England, thousands of people back home listened to the game 'live' on radio. Except there was nothing terribly live about the broadcast. The pre-recorded applause and crowd noises were added in and the 'pock' of the ball hitting the bat was made by tapping a pencil against a wooden desk in the studio.

Bradman superstats

1 Don's Test batting average was 99.94 runs an inning, making him twice as good a batsman as any other player for many years after, and no one has caught up yet.

2 His highest score in First-Class cricket was 452 runs, made in just over 400 minutes – a World Record time.

3 During his third Test match he became the youngest cricketer to score a Test century.

4 Over his career he scored 211 centuries. Of these, 41 were double centuries, 8 were triples and 1 was a quadruple century.

5 He scored 50,731 runs from 669 innings in his twenty-year career.

Career highlights

1920:   scores first century (115 not out) for Bowral High against Mittagong

1926:   invited to play with St George Cricket Club in Sydney

1927:   selected to play Sheffield Shield for the New South Wales team

1928:   selected to play his first Test for the Australian team against England

1930:   scores 452 not out for New South Wales against Queensland, a new First-Class innings record

1936:   becomes Test Captain, a position he held until 1948

1949:   receives a knighthood for services to cricket

1979:   awarded Companion of the Order of Australia (AC)

1985:   inducted into Sport Australia Hall of Fame

Peter Brock

Australia's most successful racing-car driver

Full name: Peter Geoffrey Brock

Also known as: Brocky, Peter Perfect, King of the Mountain

Born: 26 February 1945 in Hurstbridge, Victoria

Team: Mobil Holden Racing Team

Car: Holden Commodore VS **Number:** 05

Website: www.brock05.com

Early years

Peter Brock grew up in Hurstbridge, a small Victorian country town. His dad was a car mechanic, who taught him heaps about how engines worked. He first became interested in cars when he was seven, watching drivers like Jack Brabham battle it out around the old racing circuit in Altona. Both his parents encouraged him to aim high, and he spent his childhood running the fastest, jumping the farthest, and taking plenty of risks and double dares.

First break

Peter built his first racing car in the chook shed on his parents' farm. He jammed a Holden 6 3000 cc motor, gearbox and differential into the tiny body of an Austin A30. The car was dark blue with a yellow stripe down the centre, and as Peter has described it, it went 'like the clappers'. After a few successful races he was spotted by Harry Firth, who was putting together a Holden Dealer team. He asked Peter to drive in the 1969 Bathurst 500. It was Peter's first big break.

The making of a legend

Peter went on to become Australia's greatest and best known motor-sport personality. His thirty-year career has taken him all over Australia and around the world, competing in events such as the Australian and European Touring Car Championships, the Round Australia Trial and the Peter Brock Classic (which he won in 1995).

In 1997, he lined up at Bathurst for his last race and a final crack at a 'perfect 10' – ten wins in the Bathurst 1000. Unfortunately, engine failure saw his car out of the race, and Larry Perkins won.

Since Brocky hung up his helmet he has been working with young drivers in the Holden 'Young Lions' project – ensuring a whole new generation of Peter Brocks achieve their goals.

Brock superstats

1 Peter won Australia's best known motor-sport event, Bathurst 1000, a record nine times, in 1972, 1975, 1978, 1979, 1980, 1982, 1983, 1984 and 1987.
2 He also won the Sandown Endurance Race nine times, and at one stage, seven years in a row.
3 In 1997, aged fifty-two, he became the oldest driver to win an ATCC (Australian Touring Car Championship) Pole Position.

4 In twenty-five years of ATCC races he has had 205 starts resulting in 37 wins and 57 pole positions – an ATCC record.

5 His first ATCC win was Round 5 at Surfers Paradise in 1973, driving a Holden Torana GTR XU-1. His last win was Round 8 at Wanneroo in 1997, driving a Holden Commodore VS.

👉 Guess what?

For many years, Brocky has been involved with road safety and driver education. He adopted the number '05' in 1975 to highlight the government's .05 blood alcohol limit campaign. He used this number throughout his career, even though he was entitled to use the number '1' for holding the position of Australian Touring Car Champion.

Career highlights

1967:   first race at Winton Circuit, Victoria in his Austin A30

1968:   Australian Hill Climb Champion, Templestowe

1969:   first race for Holden team in the Bathurst 500

1972:   first race on ATCC circuit, at Calder Park

1976:   formed Team Brock and won his first outing

1979:   winner of Repco Round Australia Trial

1986:   drives in the European TOCA Touring Car
        Championship

1995:   wins the Peter Brock Classic at Calder Park,
        voted Motor Sports Awards 'Personality of
        the Year'

1997:   inducted into Sport Australia Hall of Fame

Robert O'Hara Burke

An explorer who was desperate to be the first European to cross Australia from south to north

Also known as: The Wild Irishman

Born: 1820 in St Clerans, County Galway, Ireland

Died: June 1861, along the banks of Cooper Creek

Website: www.burkeandwills.net

A wild youth

Robert O'Hara Burke was born in Galway in western Ireland. As a boy he loved picking fights. In his early teens, he went over to England to join the cadets. Looking for adventure, he next took off for Belgium to become a cadet in the Brussels Academy. Burke amused his new officer friends with tales of the 'wild west' back home in Ireland. When the chance came to join the Hungarian Hussars – the best cavalry regiment in Europe – he jumped at it. He did heaps of dancing, gambling, drinking, duel fighting and womanising.

Burke ran up a pile of gambling debts, and was soon facing a court martial. He quickly resigned and returned to Ireland, where he became a police officer.

☞ Guess what?

Although Burke had been chosen to lead a scientific expedition into the bush, he wasn't a scientist. Nor had he had any experience as a bushman. In fact, while he was a policeman he often got lost in the bush while on duty.

Itchy feet

Burke came out to Australia in 1853, to join the gold rush. By the time he arrived, all the good claims had been taken, so he joined the police force once again. After several jobs in Victoria he was appointed Magistrate for the Beechworth district, where he was in charge of around 40,000 miners.

Burke's sweetheart

While he was stationed at Beechworth, Burke fell for a beautiful sixteen-year-old opera singer, Julia Matthews. Every night he went to the theatre to hear her sing. He even pretended to be out searching for dangerous horse thieves so he could follow her around as she performed in different towns. Burke asked her to marry him but she knocked him back, and gave him her glove as a keepsake.

Tragedy in the outback

In 1860, Burke was asked to lead the Victorian Exploring Expedition, which aimed to cross Australia from Melbourne to the Gulf of Carpentaria. Although Burke made it through to the gulf, he never actually saw the sea. The journey back over swamps and deserts in searing heat was tough. The men were forced to eat their camels and Burke's faithful horse,

Billy. A mix of bad luck and bad judgement meant that Burke and his men missed their back-up team at Cooper Creek by only nine hours. Several days later Burke and his second-in-command, William Wills, died of starvation.

Six interesting things about Robert O'Hara Burke

1 While in the Hungarian Hussars, he fought a sabre duel with another officer over the honour of a lady.

2 When he was a police officer in Australia, he dressed like a tramp in a slouch hat, check shirt and baggy pants that lay in rolls around his heels.

3 He often dribbled spit into his long beard.

4 To annoy a magistrate in Beechworth, who hated people swinging on his front gate, Burke used to ride his horse over 20 kilometres of swamps and creeks to the magistrate's house. He'd climb up onto the gate and rattle it wildly for a few minutes, then gallop off home again.

5 Every day he bathed in a special pit he'd built at the back of his police station. He'd

lie in half a metre of rain water, stark naked except for his police helmet, and read a book.

6 He used the walls of his house as a notebook – scribbling poems, drafts of letters and notes to himself in different languages. The main message across his fireplace read, 'You are requested not to read anything on the walls.'

Career highlights

1840: becomes a cadet in the Brussels Academy, Belgium

1842: joins the Seventh Ruess Regiment of Hungarian Hussars

1848: joins Irish police

1853: appointed Acting Inspector of Melbourne Police Force

1854: appointed Police Magistrate at Beechworth

1858: appointed Police Superintendent, Castlemaine

1860: appointed Leader of the Victorian Exploring Expedition

Evonne Cawley

One of Australia's most successful tennis players, and the first Aboriginal Australian to win at Wimbledon

Full name: Evonne Fay Goolagong Cawley

Also known as: Sunshine Supergirl, Super Mum, La Belle Evonne

Born: 31 July 1951 in Barellan, New South Wales

Early years

Evonne Cawley was born in a dusty wheat town west of Sydney. She lived with her seven brothers and sisters in a tin shack with dirt floors. After school they played ball games and swam in the irrigation canal. One day, a local man saw Evonne peering through the fence of the town's tennis courts, and encouraged her to play. She was so good that the club let her join, even though she was too young. When she was ten, she told herself she was going to win Wimbledon.

The talent scout

Evonne was a natural player, with lightning reflexes. A well-known coach from Sydney, Vic Edwards, came to see her play when she was only nine. He convinced her parents to send her to Sydney for coaching lessons in the school holidays. By the age of thirteen, she had moved in with his family so the coaching could continue full-time. She began winning doubles tournaments with Vic's daughter, Patricia. By the time she was eighteen, Evonne had won thirty-seven Australian junior singles titles.

Up, up and away

Evonne made her first overseas tour as a professional player when she was nineteen. Although she won

tennis • writing

27

some minor tournaments, she was bundled out in the early rounds at Wimbledon. Then came the breakthrough. She was pitted against fellow Australian Margaret Court – at the time the best women's tennis player in the world – in the final of the Victorian Open. Evonne won. This did amazing things for her confidence. The next year she went on to win the French Open. Then, in what was probably the best game of her life, she totalled Margaret Court in two sets to take out the grand prize – Wimbledon.

Ups and downs

The next years were very uneven in terms of success. Although Evonne won four Australian titles, and was ranked among the top four tennis players in the world, she seemed to have trouble focusing on her game. She lost eight Grand Slam finals – often to her nemesis, American player Chris Evert Lloyd. Evonne married English tennis player Roger Cawley in 1975, and took time out to have her first child in 1977. In 1980, she was back at Wimbledon. This time it was Chris's turn to taste defeat as Evonne took out the title.

Game, set and match

Hamstrung by injuries, Evonne retired in 1982, at the age of thirty-one. After ten years coaching tennis in the United States, she returned to Australia. Always proud of her Aboriginal heritage, Evonne wanted her children to find out more about their culture. She is currently working with young Aboriginal athletes, and has written a book about her life.

Six amazing things about Evonne Cawley

1 Even though Evonne was incredibly successful, she never let the attention go to her head. The crowd loved her for her fresh charm and cheerful nature.

2 At the time of her first Wimbledon win, when she was nineteen, Evonne was the second youngest woman to win the singles title.

3 At the time of her second Wimbledon win, she became only the second mother in the history of the game to take out the title. The first was Dorothea Chambers in 1914.

4 Over her career, she won 92 major tournaments and every Australian mainland State singles championship.

5 As well as her many singles titles, Evonne won the doubles title at Wimbledon in

1974, and four Australian doubles titles,
in 1971, 1974, 1975 and 1976.

6 In June 2000, Evonne was the eleventh
runner to carry the Olympic torch as part
of the Sydney 2000 Olympic Games.

☞ Guess what?

Evonne's first tennis racquet was made out of
a wooden fruit box.

Career highlights

1970:   first overseas tour; plays for Australia in
Federation Cup

1971:   wins at both Wimbledon and the French
Open make her Number One in the world;
becomes Australian of the Year and Female
Athlete of the Year

1972:   awarded Member of the British Empire (MBE)

1980:   comeback win at Wimbledon

1982:   awarded Officer of the Order of Australia (AO)

1988:   inducted into the International Tennis Hall
of Fame in the USA

1997:   becomes Sports Ambassador to Aboriginal
and Torres Strait Island communities

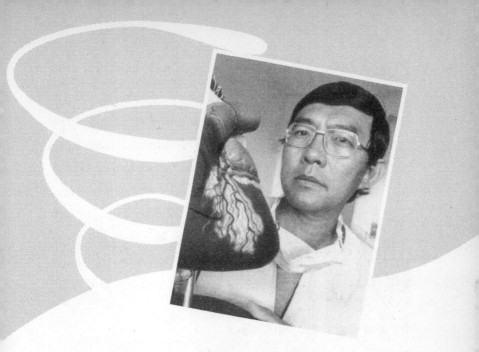

Victor Chang

The surgeon who performed Australia's first heart-lung transplant

Full name: Victor Peter Chang (Chang Yam Him)

Born: 25 November 1936 in Shanghai, China

Died: 4 July 1991 in Sydney, New South Wales

Personal motto: If you set yourself a goal it can be achieved by untiring perseverance.

Website: www.victorchang.com.au

Early years

Although Victor Chang was born in Shanghai, both his parents were Australian-born Chinese. In the first ten years of his life, his family moved home five times, settling in different parts of Asia. In 1948, when Victor was twelve, his mother died of breast cancer. She was only thirty-three. He decided that he would devote his life to becoming a doctor, helping others so that they would never have to suffer the way his mum had done.

In pursuit of a dream

Victor and his sister came to Australia three years later. They lived with their uncle in Campsie, in Sydney's western suburbs.

Victor worked hard at high school. He had to learn English before he could follow what was being taught, and started in the lowest class. Because he was really good with his hands, and loved making models of things like cars and planes, people thought he'd end up being an engineer.

But he was determined to study medicine and become a doctor.

Although he was never the top of his class, the hard work and determination to succeed paid off. Victor started medical school in 1956.

The talk that changed lives

After graduating, Victor spent a year at St Vincent's Hospital. While he was there he heard a talk by a heart surgeon that changed his life. Victor now knew what he must do – become a heart surgeon and give people back their lives. He continued his training overseas, finding out as much about heart surgery as he could.

A new challenge

In 1983, Victor set up the National Heart Transplant Centre at St Vincent's Hospital. He was always very popular with his patients due to his cheery smile and caring, positive nature. During his time there he performed 260 heart transplants. His most famous patient was fourteen-year-old Fiona Coote, who only had a few days left to live. Her heart transplant was so successful, many people were inspired to donate their organs when they died so that other people could live.

A tragic end

In 1991, Victor was working on an artificial heart. There weren't enough donated organs available to save the people who needed them. He had almost finished the project when he was shot and killed by two gunmen. They had hoped to kidnap him and force him to give them 3 million dollars, but when he refused they panicked and their plan went hopelessly wrong. A new research centre has been set up in his memory, so that his ground-breaking work can continue.

Four interesting things about Victor Chang

1 He was crazy about cars. He began making his own remote-control cars – without any plans – when he was ten. When he was sixteen, he earned pocket money fixing cars at a garage in Sydney.

2 He had a photographic memory. When studying for exams, he could read his books only a couple of times and remember the whole lot.

3 He didn't understand most of what he was taught at school for the first six months in Australia because he couldn't speak English.

4 He invented the 'bikini cut' so his patients wouldn't have to have a big chest scar after heart surgery.

Career highlights

1962: graduates from the University of Sydney as Bachelor of Surgery and Bachelor of Medicine

1964: appointed senior resident medical officer at St Vincent's Hospital, Sydney

1966: becomes a Fellow of the Royal College of Surgeons (Britain)

1973: becomes a Fellow of the Australasian College of Surgeons

1975: becomes a Fellow of the American College of Surgeons

1984: performs Australia's first successful heart transplant

1985: named Australian of the Year

1986: performs Australia's first heart-lung transplant; awarded Companion of the Order of Australia (AC)

☞ Guess what?

As a kid, Victor loved pulling things apart to see how they worked. Once he took a piano apart, but couldn't remember how to put it back together again. He copped heaps from his dad.

Caroline Chisholm

A social worker who helped women and
children in the nineteenth century

Also known as: The Emigrant's Friend

Born: 1808 in Wootton, England

Died: 25 March 1877 in London, England

Banknote: $5 (from 1967 to 1991)

Early years

Caroline was born in a farmhouse in an English village. Both her parents were kind people who helped others in the village who were doing it tough. Her dad often brought people who were down on their luck home to stay with them. Sometimes, they told the family fabulous tales about the world and their travels overseas. Caroline listened to the stories, her eyes shining. When she grew up she was determined to have adventures of her own, and help people, just as her mum and dad had done.

☞ **Guess what?**

In 1967, Caroline Chisholm became the first woman other than the Queen to appear on an Australian banknote. Her image was removed – causing public outrage – when plastic notes came into use in 1992.

Off to see the world

When she was twenty-two, Caroline fell for a good-looking army officer in his thirties. She agreed to marry him on one condition – that he never stop her from carrying out her plans to help people in need. He agreed – and kept his promise for the rest of their lives. They spent the next six years in India where Caroline had the first two of their six children. She also set up a school for the daughters of British soldiers stationed there. In 1838, the family set sail for Australia on what was meant to be a holiday.

Struggletown

When Caroline arrived in Sydney, she discovered that many girls and women were living in terrible conditions. Women had been lured over to the new colony from their homeland with the promise of a better life. But in reality, many had no jobs or homes to go to and were sleeping on the streets. Caroline realised this was her chance to make a difference. She took some of the girls home with her, trained them and found them work in her friends' homes. She also persuaded the government to set up a home for new arrivals to live in until they found work.

The emigrant's friend

Over the next thirty years, Caroline continued to help women in need. She set up employment centres in country areas, and organised work contracts so that employers treated their workers fairly. She talked to migrants about the good and bad points of coming to

Australia, then returned to Britain and gave advice to people wanting to emigrate. She helped to improve conditions for women on ships, and set up a loan scheme so that members of large families could all emigrate at the same time. When people flocked to the Victorian goldfields, she organised a series of clean, safe, cheap huts for travellers to stay in.

A sad end

Ill-health finally forced Caroline to return to England in 1866. Although she had devoted most of her life to the care and welfare of others, Caroline spent the last five years of her life poor and forgotten, stuck in bed in a dingy English house. She died in 1877, aged sixty-nine.

Three interesting things about Caroline Chisholm

I When she was young, she invented her own emigration game. She pretended that her washbasin was the ocean and her bed quilt was land. She made boats for her dolls out of broad beans. Then she'd pretend to 'transport' her dolls from one country to another by sailing them across the ocean.

2 She had plenty of male admirers to choose from and knocked back a fair few offers of marriage before she accepted the one from the man who became her husband.

3 During her first night in the Female Immigrants' Home, she met up with lots of rats. As well as the huge ones running around the floor, three climbed down from the roof and jumped on to her shoulders while she was sitting up in bed. She fed them bread laced with arsenic every night until she'd got rid of them.

Career highlights

1832: sets up a school for girls in Madras, India

1841: opens the Female Immigrants' Home in Sydney

1850: first emigrants set sail for Sydney from England funded by Caroline's Family Colonisation Society loan scheme

1854: sets up 'safe houses' for travellers to the Victorian goldfields

1862: opens a school for girls in Newtown, Sydney

Alfred Deakin

Australia's first Attorney-General and one
of the founding fathers of Federation

Also known as: Affable Alfred

Born: 3 August 1856 in Fitzroy, Victoria

Died: 7 October 1919 in South Yarra, Victoria

Early years

Alfred's parents came to Australia from England in 1849, and Alfred was born seven years later. Alfred loved reading and was a bit of a day-dreamer. After going to school at Melbourne Grammar, he studied law at Melbourne University, though without much enthusiasm. He would much rather have been a writer. Although he went on to become a lawyer, he spent as much time as he could writing poetry, essays and articles for newspapers such as the Melbourne *Age*.

☞ Guess what?

Alfred Deakin was a bit of a puzzle. Although he came across as a charming, confident person, he was actually quite insecure, with few close friends. He knocked back the offer of a knighthood because it would mean living a public life.

A new career

David Syme, the editor of the *Age* at the time, encouraged Alfred to get involved with politics in his early twenties. It seemed like a good choice for him, as Alfred was witty and charming. He loved debating, and had a rich, deep voice. He also had a way with words that made people sit up and listen. Alfred was also able to write his own speeches – something not many politicians can do, even today. He got on well with other people, and never talked down to them, no matter what background they came from. Everyone called him 'Affable Alfred'.

Towards Federation

Alfred always believed that governments should try new ideas that would help to improve people's lives. In his first years as a politician he introduced laws that improved conditions for workers in shops and factories. By the 1890s, he had a new interest – Federation. At that time, Australia was made up of six separate colonies. He thought it would be better if they all joined together to form one nation. He was so popular in his home colony – Victoria – that 80 per cent of voters agreed that Federation should take place.

Three terms

The first Federal Parliament sat on 1 January 1901. Edmund Barton, the first Prime Minister, made Alfred Attorney-General, in charge of laws and courts. When Edmund resigned as Prime Minister in 1903, Alfred took over his job. He was forty-seven years old. The next seven years were like a game of musical chairs. Alfred served three separate terms as Prime Minister, resigning twice before stepping back in again. During this time he brought about many changes that were good for Australians. These included the introduction of old age pensions and a basic wage for workers. In 1908, Canberra was chosen as the site for the nation's new capital. By 1913, Alfred was no longer well enough to continue working. He resigned from Parliament and died six years later.

Three interesting things about Alfred Deakin

1 He was interested in 'spiritualism' and believed that people could communicate with the dead through seances.
2 He used his first speech to Parliament to resign on a point of principle.
3 He liked to keep certain parts of his life secret. While he was a politician, he wrote articles about the Victorian and Australian governments for an English newspaper, using a different name. He would have been in a lot of trouble if he'd been found out, as people would think it was a conflict of

interest. He even kept it up when he became
Prime Minister, often criticising his own
actions.

Career highlights

1879: elected to the Victorian Parliament, aged
       twenty-three

1886: elected leader of the Liberal Party

1901: becomes Australia's first Attorney-General
       in the new Federal Parliament

1903–04: becomes Australia's second Prime Minister

1905–08: serves a second term as Prime Minister

1909–1910: serves a third term as Prime Minister

Edward 'Weary' Dunlop

A surgeon who took exceptional care of prisoners of war during World War II

Full name: Ernest Edward Dunlop

Also known as: Ernie, Weary, the Surgeon of the Railway

Born: 12 July 1907 in Wangaratta, Victoria

Died: 2 July 1993 in Melbourne, Victoria

Early years

When Weary Dunlop was growing up he was known as Ernie. He lived on a farm in north-eastern Victoria. Ernie and his brother loved adventure. They charged around the paddocks on horseback, taking risks and trying to prove how tough they were. Ernie was determined never to give in to pain.

☞ **Guess what?**

Edward picked up the nickname 'Weary' when he was a uni student. 'Dunlop' is a brand of tyres. His friends played on the word 'tyres', making it 'tires' – as in, someone who gets tired a lot. Tyres – tired – weary!

Before the war

Ernie was bright at school and good at sport. After studying pharmacy, he switched to medicine, graduating in 1934. While at uni, he was always looked up to by the other students. He was a born leader – good at sport and easy to get along with. When war broke out in 1939, Weary was desperate to get into the army so he could be close to the action. He joined the Australian Infantry Force Medical Corps as a surgeon.

military • medicine

War service

Weary served in north Africa, the Middle East, Greece and Crete, setting up army hospitals and caring for sick and injured soldiers. In early 1942, he was sent to Java, Indonesia to look after injured troops. Two weeks later, the hospital he was running was captured by the Japanese. Weary became a prisoner of war.

Hell on earth

The prisoners were moved from camp to camp, and suffered terrible conditions. Finally they were herded into over-crowded train carriages and taken on a five-day horror trip to Thailand. The Japanese were building a 425-kilometre railway line stretching from Thailand to Burma. The Australian prisoners of war became part of the huge team building it. They slogged through rain and mud day and night, plagued by mosquitoes, maggots and dysentery. They were only given rice to eat, and their boots rotted off their feet. One life was lost for every sleeper of the railway line that was laid.

A real hero

Weary was made their leader. It was up to him to decide who was fit enough to work – when none of them were. He led by personal example – never expecting his men to do anything he wouldn't do himself. He was also their surgeon – with no equipment or painkillers. He cut tropical ulcers out of their legs with a sharpened spoon. Sometimes, he had to remove the leg altogether. Weary stood in front of an injured man to stop him being bayoneted to death by the Japanese. He was a hero in every sense of the word.

The surgeon of the railway

After the war, Weary returned to his life as a surgeon, becoming a cancer specialist. He surprised many by having the ability to forgive and even meet up with some of his former enemies, and worked hard to improve relations between Australia and Japan. At his funeral in 1993, 10,000 people lined the streets of Melbourne. His ashes were taken back to Burma and scattered along the tracks, in memory of 'the Surgeon of the Railway'.

Four interesting things about the early life of Weary Dunlop

1 When he was kid, he and his family slept outside in a tent. His mother wanted to toughen them up so they wouldn't catch tuberculosis, a serious disease in those days.

2 He invented a world full of heroes from books and stories. He'd dress up and ride off on his horse to fight in make-believe quests.

3 He was often given the strap at school for getting in fights with his classmates.

4 When he worked in a chemist shop he was so shy he used to blush when customers asked for things like condoms or 'women's products'.

Career highlights

1934:	graduates from Melbourne University with first class honours in Medicine
1938:	becomes Fellow of the Royal College of Surgeons, London
1939:	joins Australian Army Medical Corps
1947:	awarded Officer of the Order of the British Empire (OBE)
1969:	leads a surgical team to South Vietnam during the Vietnam War
1977:	becomes Australian of the Year; receives knighthood
1987:	awarded Companion of the Order of Australia (AC)

Matthew Flinders

An explorer who drew the first detailed maps of Australia and its coastline

Born: 16 March 1774 in Donington, England

Died: 19 July 1814 in London, England

Early years

Matthew Flinders was born in a market town in Lincolnshire, England. His father and grandfather were doctors. Matthew would probably have become one too if he hadn't been given the story of Robinson Crusoe to read while at school. It made him desperate to run off to sea and have adventures of his own. When he turned fifteen he joined the Royal Navy – against the advice of his father and uncle – and trained as a navigator.

His adventures begin

When he was twenty, Matthew set sail for the new colony of Sydney on the *Reliance*, arriving in 1795. On the way out he met up with George Bass, the ship's doctor. They became good mates. The next year, they explored the coastline south of Sydney in Bass's tiny rowing boat. Bass had named it the *Tom Thumb* after the fairytale character. Their next journey took them even further south, just past where Wollongong is today. They were lucky to survive a huge wave that dumped them on the shore. Matthew's final trip with Bass took them around Van Diemen's Land (now known as Tasmania), proving it was an island. Four years later, Bass mysteriously vanished while on a trip to South America.

Charting the continent

Matthew went back to England in 1800, and married Ann Chappell the following year. He was given a boat, the HMS *Investigator*, by the British government, with orders to sail around the entire continent. He sailed back to Sydney, leaving his new wife behind. The next year, he sailed north from Sydney, following the entire length of the coastline until he arrived back where he'd started from. While he was travelling he drew charts of every bay, island or headland he came across. The journey took him just under a year.

A sticky end

The *Investigator* was now in bad shape. Many of the crew were either dead or too sick to travel again. But Matthew was keen to do some more exploring. He set off to England again to get funds for another adventure. Unfortunately, his ship, the *Cumberland,* sprang a leak on the way. He stopped at Mauritius, off the east coast of Africa, to repair it. Bad move. The French, who were at war with England, decided he was a spy. They took all his journals and charts, and threw him in jail. He stayed there, rotting, for the next six years. After his release he returned once more to England. Physically and mentally broken, he died four years later, aged only forty.

exploration • writing

Three interesting things about Matthew Flinders

1 He adopted a ship's cat, Trim, in 1799.
Cats were often kept on ships to stop rats
and mice from eating the food stores. Trim
was jet black, with white feet and a white
star on his chest. Matthew took Trim with
him on his trip around Australia, and then
back towards England on the *Cumberland*.
Some people think poor Trim probably
ended up in a stew on the island of
Mauritius. There are statues of Matthew
and Trim outside the Mitchell Library
in Sydney.

2 Once, while he was sailing along the
southern coast of New South Wales,
Matthew came across a group of Aborigines
who looked like they were about to attack
him. So he pulled out a pair of scissors
and began to cut their hair and beards.
In the meantime, George Bass got the boat
ready for a quick getaway once he'd
finished.

3 He invented names for heaps of places all
over Australia, such as Twin Peaks Islands,
Cape Knob and Lucky Bay. Other places

were named after him, for example Flinders Island in Bass Strait, the Flinders Ranges in South Australia, and Melbourne's Flinders Street and Flinders Street Station.

Career highlights

1789:   joins Royal Navy, aged fifteen

1791:   sails to Tahiti with Captain William Bligh

1795:   explores Botany Bay with George Bass

1798:   sails around Van Diemen's Land

1803:   completes journey around coast of mainland Australia

1814:   the book he wrote about his travels, *A Voyage to Terra Australis*, is published on the day he dies

☞ Guess what?

Matthew Flinders thought 'Australia' would be a good name for our country after his epic trip around its coastline. The name was finally taken up in 1817, three years after his death.

Howard Florey

A scientist who developed penicillin

Full name: Howard Walter Florey

A.k.a: Floss; the 'Bushranger of Research'

Born: 24 September 1898 in Adelaide, South Australia

Died: 21 February 1968 in Oxford, England

Website: www.tallpoppies.net.au/florey

Banknote: $50 (from 1973 to 1994)

Early years

Howard Florey was born in Adelaide at the end of the nineteenth century. His family and friends called him Floss because of his long curly hair. He was good at schoolwork, loved adventure and was a top sportsman. His favourite subject at school was chemistry. Howard dreamed of becoming a famous research scientist, such as Louis Pasteur, who discovered how germs made people sick.

On the road to fame

Howard studied medicine in Australia, then won a Rhodes Scholarship to study at Oxford in England. He became a pathologist, a person who studies diseases. People called him the 'Bushranger of Research' because he wasn't afraid to upset other people to get things done. Howard became interested in the work of Alexander Fleming. Ten years earlier, Fleming had discovered penicillin, which kills germs, but he hadn't followed up the discovery. Back in those days, if you had a scratch or cut that got infected, you might end up losing your whole limb.

Miracle worker

Howard and his research partner Ernst Chain turned penicillin into a 'wonder drug' that could kill the germs causing the infection. Since then, his work has saved the lives of more than 50 million people. Howard received many international honours, including the Nobel Prize, for his work. He died of a heart attack in 1968, aged sixty-nine.

Five fascinating facts about penicillin

1 It was discovered by accident. An English scientist, Alexander Fleming, went away on holidays for two weeks. He'd left an uncovered dish of bacteria on his desk. A spore of mould landed on the dish and began to grow. When Fleming returned the mould was the size of a twenty-cent piece, and the bacteria around it had died. Fleming didn't realise the importance of what he'd found. He chucked the dish into a bucket to be washed. Fortunately, a work friend pulled it out of the bucket when he saw the strange growth.

2 Howard's first experiments with penicillin were done on mice. Eight mice were given enough germs to kill them. Half of the diseased mice were given penicillin, and the

other half nothing. The next day, the second lot of mice were dead. But the first lot were alive and kicking. The penicillin had worked.

3 People are 3,000 times bigger than mice. So Florey needed heaps more penicillin to try out on human patients. His biggest problem was finding enough shallow containers to grow the mould in. Once he'd been through all the glass in the lab, he used things like biscuit tins, pie plates and bedpans.

4 Florey's first human patient had been scratched by a rose thorn. His body was covered with abscesses full of pus. His eye was so infected it had to be cut out. Florey gave him some penicillin. Unfortunately, Florey's supplies ran out before the man was fully cured and he died.

5 The best supplies of penicillin mould in the world came from a lab in Peoria in the United States. The tea lady – known as Mouldy Mary – brought in old socks, soggy newspapers and rotting food for the scientists to work with.

   The best penicillin came from a mouldy bit of rockmelon.

Career highlights

1921:   becomes Rhodes Scholar for South Australia

1931:   appointed Professor of Pathology at the University of Sheffield, UK

1935:   appointed Professor of Pathology at Oxford, UK

1941:   becomes Fellow of the Royal Society

1944:   receives knighthood from King George VI

1945:   shares Nobel Prize for Medicine with Ernst Chain and Alexander Fleming

1960:   becomes first Australian to be appointed President of the Royal Society of Medicine

1965:   appointed Chancellor of the Australian National University; becomes Lord Florey, Baron of Adelaide and Marston

☞ Guess what?

Howard's wife, Ethel, was a big help in his research. She rode her bike from the hospital to his research lab, carrying bottles of patients' penicillin-filled pee.

Errol Flynn

An actor who scandalised Hollywood with his swashbuckling ways

Full name: Errol Leslie Thomson Flynn

Born: 20 June 1909 in Hobart, Tasmania

Died: 14 October 1959 in Vancouver, Canada

Website: www.inlikeflynn.com

Early years

Errol Flynn's father was a marine biologist and zoologist who studied animals at the Hobart Zoo. Young Errol was a bit of a naughty boy. He was expelled from every school he went to, and failed all his exams. His first taste of showbiz came performing in a pantomime at Hobart's Theatre Royal, along with other students from Miss Lola Smith's Dancing Class.

What Errol did next

During his late teens and early twenties Errol lived a racy life, involving himself in gold prospecting, slave-trading and diamond-smuggling. He was naturally sporty and loved sailing. Together with a group of friends, he spent seven months sailing to New Guinea. His big break came when the wife of famous movie director Charles Chauvel spotted Errol's muscles while he was strutting his stuff on Bondi Beach. Charles offered him the part of Fletcher Christian in a film called *In the Wake of the Bounty*.

Hollywood

Errol arrived in Hollywood in 1935, after a year of stage performances in England. After two small parts, he hit the big time with *Captain Blood*, where he got to play a swashbuckling pirate and fight lots of duels. Suddenly Errol was an overnight sensation. With his startling good looks, dazzling charm and sporty physique he was soon being cast as the hero in all sorts of action movies – westerns, costume dramas, war epics. Audiences couldn't get enough of him. Meanwhile he was drinking hard and playing around off screen as much as on – and not just tennis. He married three times (his second wife was only eighteen when they married – he was mid-30s), and managed to fit in plenty of affairs as well, fuelling the Hollywood gossip columns.

Seven things Errol Flynn really, really liked

1 women
2 the sea
3 writing and reading
4 freaking people out
5 his dog, Arno
6 women
7 the sea

The end of a legend

Eventually, Errol's body failed to keep up with his devil-may-care lifestyle. His last movie, *Cuban Rebel*

Girls, was a Z-grade dud. Although he had starred in more than fifty movies, he never won any awards or gained any serious recognition for his work. He died in 1959 from a heart attack, aged only fifty – but looking much older.

Five fascinating things about Errol Flynn

1   He was one of the best sword-fighters in Hollywood, and never used a body double or stuntman the way other actors did.

2   In 1941 he lost his beloved dog and best friend, Arno, a five-year-old schnauzer. Arno was swept overboard his boat, the *Sirocco*. Some people say Errol never recovered from the loss.

3   Errol had four kids. His son, Sean, was a dead ringer for his dad. He went missing – presumed dead – in 1970 while he was working as a photo-journalist and war correspondent in South-East Asia.

4   He wrote three books. The third book, *My Wicked, Wicked Ways*, told his life story.

5 He loved brawling and went out of his way to start a fight.

Famous Flynn movies

In the Wake of the Bounty (1933) Errol's first film
Captain Blood (1935)
The Charge of the Light Brigade (1936)
The Adventures of Robin Hood (1938)
Dodge City (1939)
The Sea Hawk (1940)
They Died with their Boots On (1941)
The Adventures of Don Juan (1949)

Guess what?

The expression 'in like Flynn' comes from Errol's legendary ability to charm women.

John Flynn

Founder of the Royal Flying Doctor Service

Also known as: Flynn of the Inland

Born: 25 November 1880 in Moliagul, Victoria

Died: 5 May 1951 in Sydney, New South Wales

Website: www.rfds.org.au

Banknote: $20

Early years

John Flynn was born on the Victorian goldfields in 1880. His mum died when he was only two. John and his brother and sister were brought up by their strict school-teacher father. Thomas Flynn was very religious, and the kids all went to Bible Class, where John loved listening to tales about the outback.

Tough times

After working for a while as a teacher, John decided to train to become a minister. When he was twenty-nine he was sent to work as a missionary in Beltana, in northern South Australia. It didn't take him long to realise that people living in the outback were doing it tough. There were no telephones back then, and people lived long distances from shops or medical assistance. He collected books and magazines for lonely farmers, and often treated sick or injured people from his own first-aid chest.

The inland mission

John was asked to write a report on how the church could help people living in the bush. He travelled around the outback, asking people for ideas. He did such a good job, the church leaders set up a program called the Australian Inland Mission, and made him head of it. He and a group of ministers, known as 'Flynn's Mob', helped set up fifteen hospitals and worked hard to make the bush the sort of place people could bring their families to.

> ☞ **Guess what?**
>
> The Reverend John Flynn has had more memorials dedicated to him than any other Australian.

The sad story of Jimmy Darcy

In 1917, a stockman named Jimmy Darcy was seriously hurt when he fell from his horse. He was 500 kilometres from the closest doctor. His friends carried him 50 kilometres to the nearest town, Halls Creek. The postmaster there got in touch with a doctor in Perth by morse code, who tapped out instructions for the badly needed operation. Jimmy got sicker and sicker. It took the doctor thirteen days to get there by boat, car and buggy – only to find that Jimmy had died the day before. When John heard the awful story he realised that unless something was done to bring medical help to people living in remote areas, more people could die needlessly.

The RFDS is born

John told Jimmy's story as he travelled around Australia. Soon he had enough support to set up what was to become the Royal Flying Doctor Service. Planes brought doctors and nurses to patients in remote areas. John also helped set up a system of pedal-powered radios that allowed people to call for medical help – or just chat with their friends. His magazine, *The Inlander*, kept people informed of all the latest news. John died of cancer in 1951, aged seventy-one. His ashes were buried in a special grave near Alice Springs.

Three interesting things about John Flynn

1 He was very good with his hands. While travelling around the outback as a minister, helping to mend people's souls, he also mended things that had broken down. He was especially good at fixing watches and clocks.

2 He put together a best-selling book called *The Bushman's Companion*. It gave people living in the outback hints on how to make a will, handle their money and accounts, and how to hold a funeral service.

3 He set up a pen-friend scheme so that lonely people in the bush could write to people in the city.

Career highlights

1911: first appointment as a minister

1912: appointed Superintendent of the Australian Inland Mission

1913: begins publishing his magazine, *The Inlander*

1928: first official flight of Flynn's aerial medical service leaves Cloncurry for Julia Creek

1933: appointed Officer of the Order of the British Empire (OBE)

1934: Australian Aerial Medical Service set up (its name was later changed to Royal Flying Doctor Service)

1939: elected Moderator-General of the Presbyterian Church of Australia

Dawn Fraser

An Olympic champion considered to be the world's best-ever female swimmer

Full name: Dawn Lorraine Fraser

Also known as: Our Dawn

Born: 4 September 1937 in Balmain, New South Wales

Personal motto: Once you set your mind to do anything you can do it.

Website: www.dawnfraser.com.au

Early years

Dawn grew up in the inner suburbs of Sydney, the youngest of eight children. Dawn was always a sporty, cheeky kid. She left school at fourteen because she didn't like being told what to do. Her brother Don started taking her to the pool when she was six to help her overcome her breathing problems, caused by asthma. Dawn loved swimming and soon began to win races, cheered on by Don.

Record breaker

Don died of leukaemia when Dawn was thirteen. She was determined to keep up her training, in his memory. By the time she was fifteen she was swimming like a champion. Swimming coach Harry Gallagher offered to train her for free, and she joined his squad.

Dawn went on to break several Australian women's freestyle swimming records. Her first world record came in 1956, when she swam the 100 yards freestyle in 64.5 seconds at the Melbourne Olympic Games.

Our Dawn

Everyone loved 'our Dawn'. She was admired for her courage and determination to win, even though she suffered many setbacks during her career. Both her parents died when she was still quite young. Ever the larrikin, she often found herself in trouble. After her triumph at the Tokyo Games in 1964, where she became the first swimmer in history to win an event at three consecutive games, she was banned from swimming for ten years. The officials said she had marched in the opening ceremony against orders, worn the wrong swimsuit and – horror of horrors – had stolen a Japanese flag from the Emperor's palace with a group of other athletes. The ban was lifted after four years, but her career was over.

Three amazing things about Dawn Fraser

1 During her early years of training she often used to swim with her legs tied together, dragging a four-gallon drum behind her, to help strengthen her arm strokes.

2 Just before the 1964 Tokyo Games, Dawn's mum was killed in a car accident. Dawn was the driver. Even though she was injured herself, Dawn went to the Games, believing her mum would have wanted her to. She set a new record of 59.5 seconds for her event and made swimming history by winning her third gold in a row.

3 At the 1956 Melbourne Olympic Games, she waited till she was sure the Russian swimmers were looking at her, then took some headache tablets. Then she whizzed down the practice pool, much faster then her normal practice times. The Russians fell for her trick – convinced that she was taking illegal drugs to improve her performance.

After the games

Since she retired from swimming, Dawn has worked as a swimming coach, and been a member of the New South Wales parliament. She has been honoured many times over the years for her legendary ability and spirit. In 1999, she was named one of Australia's National Living Treasures.

☞ Guess what?

One time, Dawn's brothers' school football team was a player short. They grabbed a pair of scissors, cut her hair to make her look like a boy, and dressed her up in footy gear. She played the whole match.

Dawn Fraser superstats

World records: 39 (27 individual, 12 team)
Australian titles: 30 (23 individual, 7 team)
Olympic gold medals
100 m freestyle (1956, 1960, 1964)
4 × 100 m relay (1956)
Olympic silver medals
400 m freestyle (1956, 1964)
4 × 100 m freestyle relay (1960)
4 × 100 m medley relay (1960)
Commonwealth Games medals: 6 gold, 2 silver

Career highlights

1955:	wins her first big race
1956:	breaks the longest standing world record for the 100-metre freestyle; swims in her first Olympic Games
1964:	becomes the first swimmer to win the same event at three consecutive Olympic Games
1967:	becomes Member of the Order of the British Empire (OBE)
1983:	voted Australia's greatest ever Olympian
1988:	voted Australia's greatest female athlete
1999:	named World Sports 'Greatest Female Swimmer of the Century'

Cathy Freeman

A champion sprinter and the first Aboriginal runner to represent Australia at the Olympic Games

Full name: Catherine Astrid Salome Freeman

Born: 16 February 1973 in Mackay, Queensland

Website: www.cathyfreeman.com.au

Early years

Cathy Freeman grew up in a dusty town in outback Queensland. Her family was poor, and there was never enough money for food and clothes. Both her dad, known as 'Twinkle Toes', and her grandad were rugby legends.

Cathy and her four brothers were all good at sport as well. When Cathy's Grade 1 teacher encouraged her to run in a race on school sports day, she was hooked. By the time she was eight she had won her first gold medal – at the State Primary School Athletics Championships in Brisbane.

Training

During her childhood, Cathy often came up against racist attitudes, both from people in her home town and in the sporting world. When she was ten, she won most of her races at an inter-school championship in Mt Isa. However, medals were only handed out to the white kids. It didn't stop Cathy's determination to keep running – and be the best. Her stepfather, Bruce Barber, trained Cathy and her brother Norman himself, even though he had no experience.

After the medals kept coming, the family moved several times so Cathy could get the best coaching possible. They raised money through lamington drives and cake stalls to send her to the Pacific Games, and even to California.

A brilliant career

Cathy's first international gold medal was at the 1990 Commonwealth Games, when she was sixteen. She made the finals at the 1992 Olympic Games in Barcelona, and took out silver for the 400 metres at the 1996 Atlanta Games, becoming the sixth fastest woman ever over that distance. Earlier that year, Cathy became the first Australian woman to run the 400 metres in under fifty seconds. In 1997, after her win in the 400 metres at the World Track and Field Championships, she was ranked number one in the world.

☞ Guess what?

After her winning race at the Commonwealth Games in 1994, Cathy caused a media stir by wrapping herself in the Aboriginal and Australian flags to run her lap of honour. Some sporting officials were angry because the Aboriginal flag was not in official use at that time. She did it again after her Olympic gold in 2000 – to the delight of the crowd!

Setbacks and rivals

Cathy's road to success hasn't always been an easy one. Injury kept her out of the 1998 Commonwealth Games. When she broke up with her boyfriend and manager, Nick Bideau, the media gave her a hard time. But Cathy kept her focus and managed to stay cool. Then her biggest rival, French runner Marie-Jo Perec, came to Sydney for the 2000 Olympics. When she suddenly returned home, giving no explanation, Cathy never let the pressure get to her. Not even when she knew the whole of the country was counting on her to win that race. She ran the race of her life, and became Australia's golden girl.

What Cathy did next

Cathy took time out from her career in 2001 to follow other interests. She lived with her new husband, Sandy Bodecker, in America, learnt Italian, and worked for a newspaper that helped homeless people. By 2002 she was ready to get back into training. However, a leg injury threw her schedule out of whack. When Sandy was diagnosed with throat cancer, looking after him became her first priority. With his encouragement, she made it to Manchester and her fourth Commonwealth gold medal. Sandy made a complete recovery, however Cathy and Sandy split in 2003 for personal reasons.

Cathy Freeman superstats

Personal best times

100 m 11.24 seconds

200 m 22.25 seconds

400 m 48.63 seconds

Gold medals

4 × 100 m relay (1990 Commonwealth Games)

200 m (1994 Commonwealth Games)

400 m (1994 Commonwealth Games)

400 m (2000 Olympic Games)

4 × 400 m relay (2002 Commonwealth Games)

Silver medal

400 m (1996 Olympic Games)

Awards and honours

1990:   Young Australian of the Year; Aboriginal
        Athlete of the Year

1996:   Telstra Sports Personality of the Year

1997:   Telstra Female Athlete of the Year;
        Aboriginal and Torres Strait Islander
        Sportswoman of the Year

1998:   Australian of the Year

2000:   Chosen to light the flame at the Sydney
        Olympic Games

May Gibbs

A writer and illustrator who created the Gumnut Babies, Snugglepot and Cuddlepie

Full name: Cecilia May Gibbs

Pen names: Blob, Stan Cottman

Born: 17 January 1877 in Sydenham, England

Died: 27 November 1969 in Sydney, New South Wales

Website: www.maygibbs.com.au

Early years

May was born in southern England in 1877. When she was four her family moved out to Australia – first to a farm north of Adelaide, then to an estate called 'The Homestead' at Harvey in Western Australia. May and her brothers went on long walks through the bush, looking at flowers and birds' nests and swimming in the river. Although May loved painting and drawing, what she really wanted to be was an actress. Her first picture was published in a Perth newspaper when she was twelve.

To London and back

After working for a while as an illustrator for the *Western Mail*, May went back to England to attend art school in London, where her parents had studied. When she returned to Australia in 1913, she became the first qualified full-time children's book illustrator in the country. Her first works were covers for books and newspapers, and illustrations for other people's books. But before long she began to create her own books, full of gumnut babies and flower children.

A love of the bush

May's illustrations were based on her childhood memories of the bush around the Harvey River, where her family had once lived. Her books had sweet titles, such as *Little Ragged Blossom*, or *The Adventures of Snugglepot and Cuddlepie*. But her chubby, cheeky, no-nonsense characters were very different from the elegant fairies found in European fairytales. The Gumnut Babies and the ugly, evil Banksia Men were cut out for a life in the bush filled with adventure and danger. Australian children loved them.

A life's work

May married Bertram James Ossoli Kelly in 1919, and they built a beautiful house and garden on Sydney Harbour, called Nutcote. During her long career (she worked well into her eighties), May created weekly comic strips, wrote and illustrated more than thirty books, drew illustrations for school magazines and readers, and created political cartoons. In 1955, she received an MBE (Member of the British Empire) for her services to Australian literature. Nutcote is now a museum dedicated to her life and work.

☞ Guess what?

May's comic strip, 'Bib and Bub', appeared in various newspapers for more than forty years.

Three interesting things about May Gibbs

1 Her first children's story, written in 1905, was called *Minnie and Wog, Their Adventures in Australia.* May showed it to publishers in England, but they weren't interested in stories set in the Australian bush. So she rewrote the book and gave it a new name – *About Us.* Instead of bush creatures, she wrote about chimney-pot people living on the rooftops of London.

2 She drew pictures of Australian animals and birds to go on the postcards and calendars given to homesick Australian soldiers fighting overseas in World War I.

3 You can see 2000 of her watercolours and sketches at the Mitchell Library in Sydney, or visit her house and garden at Nutcote.

Five books by May Gibbs

Gum Blossom Babies (1916)

Snugglepot and Cuddlepie (1918)

Chucklebud and Wunkydoo (1924)

Bib and Bub, Their Adventures (1927)

Prince Dande Lion: A Garden Whim Wham (1953)

Percy Grainger

Thought to be one of the best composers of the twentieth century

Full name: George Percy Grainger (later changed to Percy Aldridge Grainger)

Also known as: Bubbles; The Jogging Pianist

Born: 8 July 1882 in Brighton, Victoria

Died: 20 February 1961 in White Plains, New York, USA

Early years

Percy Grainger's dad was a well-known architect, who drew up the plans for the Princes Bridge in Melbourne. He called Percy 'Bubbles' because, with his golden curls and blue eyes, he looked like the little boy in a famous soap commercial. When he was five, Percy's mother Rose started to teach him to play the piano. Rose was very strict, and Percy spent hours every day practising and studying, instead of playing with other kids. He was so lonely he invented an imaginary friend to talk to, called Shot-a-tee. Rose also encouraged him to draw and paint, and to read aloud every day. He loved stories about early English history and invasions by the Vikings.

Off to Europe

By the time he was ten, Percy was so good at the piano that Rose sent him off to have lessons from a famous German musician living in Melbourne. The next year, he played his first concert at the Melbourne Masonic Hall. A music critic raved about his performance, predicting fame and fortune for the young pianist. When he was thirteen Rose took Percy to Germany to study piano and composition from some of the best teachers in Europe. By the time he was eighteen Percy was famous. The music critic had been right.

Country folk tunes

Percy was never a snob about music. He always thought that popular music, such as the songs and ditties people sang in the pub or the fields, was just as important as the classical music played in grand concert halls. He toured around the countryside, listening to and recording different tunes. These tunes had a big influence on many of his own compositions, such as 'Country Gardens' and 'Molly on the Shore'.

☞ Guess what?

Once, while on tour in South Africa, Percy spent the whole night walking to the next town. He was late for his concert, so his friends came out to look for him. The next thing they saw was a group of fierce-looking Zulu warriors charging towards them, with Percy jogging along behind. He'd hoped to invite them to his concert.

America and beyond

In 1914, Percy migrated to the United States, but he always made the time to come back to play in Australia. He married Ella Strom, a Swedish artist, in 1928. During his long career Percy wrote or arranged over 1200 pieces of music. He was always ahead of his time, and towards the end of his life became keen on experimental, or 'free' music, where machines played the notes. He died of stomach cancer in New York, aged seventy-eight.

Five interesting things about Percy Grainger

1 He kept his curly hair blond throughout most of his life by dyeing it with hydrogen peroxide.

2 He was always very close to his mother. Several of his girlfriends broke up with him because they thought he paid more attention to his mum than he did to them.

3 He instructed that, after his death, his bones be preserved and displayed in the museum he founded in Melbourne. (This request wasn't taken up, and he was buried in a grave in South Australia.)

4 Percy loved exercise and kept his body fit by walking and running whenever he could. He soon became known as the 'jogging pianist'. He'd jog from his hotel into concert halls in his running shorts, with his dinner suit

stuffed into his backpack. Rather than travel by train from town to town on a concert tour, he'd walk or jog there, avoiding stray dogs that snapped at his ankles.

5 He had his own eccentric style when it came to clothing. He bought his undies, boots and socks at army surplus stores. Although in those days it was unthinkable not to wear a hat in public, he refused to wear one. He was arrested twice by police officers who thought he was a tramp because he wasn't wearing a hat.

Five of Percy's compositions

Country Gardens
Spoon River
Lincolnshire Posy
Handel in the Strand
To a Nordic Princess

Germaine Greer

A writer and academic whose books have helped change women's lives around the world

Born: 29 January 1939 in Elwood, Victoria

Growing up

Germaine grew up in Melbourne, and went to a Catholic girls' school in Gardenvale. She enjoyed school and learning different languages. She ran away from home twice because she was so desperately unhappy there. There was never any music, art, flowers or books, all things that she craved, in her home. Many years later, after her father died, Germaine wrote a book about her childhood, called *Daddy, We Hardly Knew You*.

Student life

Germaine won a scholarship to study English and French Literature at Melbourne University. Then it was on to Sydney University, where she took out a Master of Arts degree. In Sydney she joined a free-thinking group of people called 'the Push', who hung out in inner-city pubs, talking about what was wrong with society and family values. In 1964, she won a scholarship to Cambridge University in England, where she studied the early writing of Shakespeare, acted in plays and wrote articles for student newspapers. In 1967, Germaine became a lecturer at Warwick University. She continued to write in-your-face articles about equal rights and sexual freedom for women, and appeared on TV and radio chat shows.

writing • feminism • activism

The Female Eunuch

Germaine's best known book, *The Female Eunuch*, was published in 1970. It pointed out that, in both the workplace and the home, men were getting a much better deal than women. It encouraged women who were miserable to change their lives to suit themselves, rather than do what society expected them to do. The book caused a storm all over the world, and became an instant best-seller. Germaine was now even more in demand to talk to the media and public about women's liberation. Many people attacked her, calling her a man-hater, and accused her of wanting to destroy society and the family.

A writing life

Over the years, Germaine continued to write books about women and their lives. *The Obstacle Race* looked at the problems female artists faced. *Sex and Destiny* compared the lives of women from different countries around the world. A collection of her essays, *The Madwoman's Underclothes*, came out in 1990. Thirty years after *The Female Eunuch*, Germaine decided it was time to get angry again. *The Whole Woman* argues that women are still getting a raw deal compared with men in terms of the work they do, and looks at the state of the feminist movement today.

Four interesting things about Germaine Greer

1 She was thrown out of her class at school for disagreeing with a nun who said that communism was the devil's work.

2 In 1968 she married Paul de Feu, an English journalist, but the marriage broke up three weeks later.

3 In 2000, a uni student from Bath broke into her home, tied her up and smashed up all her stuff with a fire poker. She didn't like what Germaine had been writing about in her books.

4 While researching her book *The Obstacle Race*, Germaine spent eight years wandering round art galleries in Europe, searching for a great undiscovered female artist.

Six books by Germaine Greer

The Female Eunuch (1970)

The Obstacle Race: The Fortunes of Women Painters and their Work (1979)

Sex and Destiny: The Politics of Human Fertility (1984)

Daddy, We Hardly Knew You (1989)

The Madwoman's Underclothes (1990)

The Whole Woman (1999)

Fred Hollows

An eye doctor who gave back sight to thousands of underprivileged people from all over the world

Full name: Frederick Cossom Hollows

Born: 9 April 1929 in Dunedin, New Zealand

Died: 10 February 1993 in Sydney, New South Wales

Website: www.hollows.com.au

Early years

Fred was born in Dunedin, a wintry city on the South Island of New Zealand. His dad was an engine driver, and Fred loved riding up next to him in the cabin. Fred was always interested in machinery and how things worked. When he was seven, the family moved to a farm at Palmerston North. Fred's dad was very religious, and Fred caught the religion bug too. He taught Bible classes and went off to camps run by the Boys' Brigade. By the time he'd finished school he'd decided to become a minister.

A change of course

While Fred was studying at Bible college he did some holiday work at a psychiatric hospital. It changed his life. He'd already begun to have doubts about becoming a minister. Now he realised that there were more practical ways of being kind and helpful to people. He changed his course to medicine instead, specialising in eye surgery in England. Fred came to Australia in 1960. Five years later he became head of the Eye Department at a Sydney hospital.

The larrikin saint

While travelling around Australia, Fred discovered that many Aboriginal people living in outback communities had an eye disease called trachoma, caused by poor health. If it was left untreated, the people became blind. During the 1970s, he helped set up a national program to overcome the problem. He inspired other doctors to give their time for free. Teams of medical staff went to the outback, treating 30,000 people, performing over 1000 operations and prescribing over 10,000 pairs of glasses. People began to call Fred – who loved the bush but had a wild temper – the 'larrikin saint' and the 'wild colonial boy' of Australian surgery.

Around the world

In the 1980s, Fred travelled to developing countries around the world to help set up programs to deal with eye disease. Millions of people in Africa and Asia were going blind every year, when the disease was actually preventable. He trained local doctors to perform simple eye operations and helped set up a factory to make special lenses that help restore sight.

His work continues

Fred married one of his students and co-workers, Gabi O'Sullivan, in 1980. They had five children together. When Fred realised he was dying of cancer, he and Gabi set up the Fred Hollows foundation so that his work could continue. Thousands of mourners, including people from Nepal, Vietnam and Eritrea, turned up to Bourke, in far-western New South Wales, to attend his funeral.

Five interesting things about Fred Hollows

1 He loved mountain-climbing.

2 People often called him a 'stirrer' because of his very strong views and opinions. But Fred thought the name just showed that he was doing his job properly.

3 He never dressed in a suit like other doctors, preferring shorts and open-necked shirts.

4 He occasionally 'borrowed' drugs and medical equipment from the hospital he was working in to stock the Aboriginal Medical Service he set up in Sydney.

5 The hospital he worked at in Eritrea was actually a secret rocky valley. The patients were treated in caves that had been hacked out by hand, and make-shift offices and storerooms were hidden under the branches of trees. It was built like this to keep it safe from attacks by the Ethiopian Air Force.

Career highlights

1965: appointed Professor of Ophthalmology at the University of New South Wales

1990: awarded Australian of the Year; awarded Australian Human Rights Medal

1991: awarded Companion of the Order of Australia (AC); Humanist of the Year

1993: receives Rotary International Award for World Understanding

☞ Guess what?

When Fred asked Australians to help provide funds to build an eye lens factory in Eritrea, they donated over 6 million dollars.

Barry Humphries

The entertainer lurking within housewife superstar, Dame Edna Everage

Full name: John Barry Humphries

Born: 17 February 1934 in Camberwell, Victoria

Website: www.dame-edna.com

Early years

Barry Humphries grew up in a neat, leafy suburb of Melbourne, where people always made sure they were nice and did things properly because they were worried about what the neighbours might think. At school, he had a reputation for being a bit of a show-off. He won prizes for his poetry and paintings, and drew funny pictures of his teachers on the blackboard. But it was in school plays that he really shone, especially when he played the part of a woman.

Out to shock

Barry always liked to stand out from the crowd, and loved playing practical jokes and shocking people. In his final years at school he became interested in abstract art and experimental music. While studying arts and law at Melbourne University in the 1950s, he spent most of his time acting in student revues or putting on his own art shows. They featured items called 'Pus in Boots' (which was an army boot filled with custard) and 'Now We Are Sick' (a bucket filled with stuff that looked like vomit).

Dame Edna is born

After two years at uni, Barry dropped out to become an actor. While travelling around country towns, his most famous character, Dame Edna Everage, was

theatre • music • writing • tv • movies

born. He used to entertain the other actors on the tour bus by sending up the wives of the mayors of the country towns they played in. Then, in 1955, daggy housewife Edna Everage from Moonee Ponds appeared on stage for the first time, in a Christmas revue at a Melbourne theatre.

> ☞ Guess what?
>
> Barry Humphries' first job was at the record company EMI. He was given a hammer and told to smash up all the old 78 records, which were to be replaced with the new, lighter, long-playing versions, known as 33s.

Barry in London

Barry left Australia for London in 1959. He acted in plays such as *Oliver!* and put together his own one-man show, which was a roaring success. He created a comic strip called *The Adventures of Barry McKenzie*, about a foul-mouthed boozy ocker Australian living in London. Two films based on the comic were made in the 1970s. In the second film, *Barry McKenzie Holds His Own*, the Prime Minister at the time, Gough Whitlam, made Edna Everage a Dame. Her official title now became 'Dame Edna, Housewife Superstar'. She starred in theatres all over Australia and England, waving a bunch of gladdies (gladioli) and welcoming the crowd with the words, 'Hello, Possums!'.

Sandy and Les

Besides Dame Edna, Barry created two other popular characters. Sandy Stone is a sad old man who likes wearing cardigans and going to the bingo and the RSL for a 'nice night's entertainment'. Sir Les Patterson is a disgusting drunk who dribbles all over his dinner suit while telling the audience all the terrible things he's got up to as Australia's Cultural Attaché. Barry has also written several books through the eyes of his characters, and two autobiographies. His most recent success has been in America, where he performs sell-out tours of his stage shows. Dame Edna continues to be an incredibly gifted and famous jet-setting megastar, with appearances before crowned royalty and on the popular TV show, 'Ally McBeal'.

Three interesting things about Barry Humphries

1   His school magazine rejected one of his poems because it was so good the teachers

thought it would put all the other kids off contributing anything themselves.

2 He gets very nervous before a show, and sometimes forgets his lines.

3 During his student days, he loved playing practical jokes while travelling on public transport. He'd sit on a tram wearing six-toed gloves on his feet, just to see the other passengers' reactions.

Five books by Barry Humphries

Bazza Holds his Own (1974)
Dame Edna's Bedside Companion (1982)
The Traveller's Tool, Sir Les Patterson (1985)
The Life and Death of Sandy Stone (1990)
My Life as Me (2002)

Paul Jennings

One of Australia's most successful and best-loved writers for kids

Full name: Paul Arthur Jennings

Born: 30 April 1943 in Heston, England

Website: www.pauljennings.com

Early years

Paul was born in Heston, west of London. His mum and dad both worked in a tool-making factory. When Paul was six, his family climbed aboard the S.S. *Ranchi* and sailed to Australia. They settled in Moorabbin, and Paul went to Bentleigh West Primary School. He had a very strict, mean teacher in Grade 5, but a wonderful teacher in Grade 6. These days, when he writes about nice teachers in his stories, he remembers things about his Grade 6 teacher, Mr Wheeler.

After school

Paul was a good writer at school. He wrote his first short story when he was sixteen, and sent it off to the *Women's Weekly*. When the magazine didn't buy it, he was very disappointed. After he finished school, Paul worked as a teacher in primary schools and at a youth training centre in Melbourne. He then trained to be a teacher of disabled children and a speech pathologist, helping people who had speech problems such as stuttering. Later, Paul became a lecturer in special education and language and literature.

Unreal

When Paul's eleven-year-old son complained that the book he was reading was boring, Paul decided to see if he could write a better story himself. He thought kids would like stories that were interesting and entertaining, with a surprise ending. He sent three of his stories to a publisher, who asked him to write five more. In 1985, *Unreal*, his first book, came out. Kids from all over the country sent him letters, telling him how much they liked his stories.

Story ideas

When asked where he gets his ideas from, Paul says that the boy in many of his books is actually him. He remembers funny, sad or embarrassing things that happened to him when he was a kid and weaves these into his stories. Since *Unreal*, Paul has written more than thirty books, including picture books and two series, *Wicked!* and *Deadly!*, with Morris Gleitzman. He has also written scripts for the TV series 'Round the Twist', and a movie script based on the *Gizmo* books. In 1995, he received an Officer of the Order of Australia award (AO) for his services to literature.

Eight interesting things about Paul Jennings

l   On his first day of school, he went home at playtime because he didn't like it. The teacher brought him back to school and made him stand out the front and apologise to the other kids.

2   He loved reading when he was a kid, especially the *William* books by Richmal Crompton. He used to read them to his sister Ruth by torchlight.

3   He used to have to collect wheelbarrows full of stinky horse manure to put on his family's vegetable garden. He writes about this in his story 'Cow-dung Custard'.

4   He was a bit of a naughty boy at high school. He used to fire up the other kids to make stink bombs. They'd put wattle seeds inside jars, then spit on them and quickly screw on the lid. Then they'd all take the lids off at the same time and stink out the classroom.

5   He once encouraged a stray dog that was hanging around his classroom to come in by putting some of his lunch on the floor. The dog scooted inside through the teacher's legs, then ran around causing chaos for the next ten minutes.

6   He once used his dad's toothbrush to groom his pet mice.

7 He loves collecting and driving classic cars.

8 He can see whales from the windows of his house set into the cliffs at Warrnambool, on Victoria's southern coast.

Ten books by Paul Jennings

Unreal (1985)

Uncanny (1988)

The Cabbage Patch Fib (1989)

The Paw Thing (1989)

Grandad's Gifts (1992)

Duck for Cover (1994)

The Gizmo (1994)

Wicked! (with Morris Gleitzman) (1997)

Singenpoo Strikes Again (1998)

Tongue-Tied! (2002)

☞ Guess what?

So far, Paul Jennings has sold 6.7 million copies of his books and has won dozens of awards for his writing, including the kids' choice YABBA and KOALA awards.

Daniel Johns

The lead singer and songwriter of silverchair

Full name: Daniel Paul Johns

Also known as: Johnsy, Jasper

Born: 22 April 1979 in Merewether, Newcastle, New South Wales

Website: www.chairpage.com; www.silverchair.nu

Early years

Daniel grew up in the surf suburb of Merewether, in Newcastle. He played trumpet in the school band, took breakdancing classes and wrote rap songs with his best friend, Ben Gillies, who he'd known since he was five. When Daniel was eleven his father played him one of his old Black Sabbath records. He was so impressed by Tony Iommi's guitar riffs he decided to play guitar himself. His first guitar was a Rocks Axe, and he used to sit in his room, working out how to play riffs by Tony Iommi or Ritchie Blackmore from Deep Purple.

From garage to radio

Daniel's first band was called Short Elvis, because they only played covers of Elvis songs. When he was twelve, Daniel started jamming with his friends Ben and Chris in his garage after school. They formed a band called the Innocent Criminals, and began playing around the local clubs. Two years later, they sent a demo tape into a band competition run by youth radio station Triple J, and Nomad, an SBS TV show. Their original song, 'Tomorrow', beat 800 other entries and scored them a recording contract. The band changed its name to silverchair, and released 'Tomorrow' in August 1994. The song became an instant hit, spending six weeks at number one on the Australian singles chart. The next year it became the most played song of 1995 on rock radio in the United States.

A star student

'Frogstomp', silverchair's first album, was recorded in nine days, when Daniel was only fifteen. It became an instant hit, both locally and overseas. Daniel juggled schoolwork with rock stardom, touring the United States with the Red Hot Chili Peppers. The next year his second album, 'Freak Show', was released. Once again, Daniel had to fit in world tours while studying for his final school exams.

☞ Guess what?

Daniel's band's fan club is known as The Llama Appreciation Society.

Health battles

Over the next few years, Daniel battled various health problems, including an eating disorder and depression. Throughout this time he continued to write edgy and thoughtful songs for silverchair's third album, 'Neon Ballroom'. In 2002, the band was forced to cancel tours and shows to promote their fourth album, 'Diorama', when Daniel was struck down by reactive arthritis. Painful, swollen joints meant he was unable to move around, play or even hold his guitar. After a nine-month battle he recovered in time to play at the 2002 ARIA (Australian Record Industry Association) awards. In early 2003, he became engaged to singer Natalie Imbruglia.

Six interesting things about Daniel Johns

1 He is a vegan, which means he does not use or eat any animal products, and disagrees with the use of animals in experimental testing.

2 While he was touring with the Red Hot Chili Peppers in America, he was arrested for driving a sports car on a Santa Monica beach, without a licence. His record company fixed everything up, however, and he ended up signing autographs for the arresting officer's daughter.

3 He collects rare and vintage guitars and owns more than twenty of them.

4 When he was twelve he became obsessed with 1960s band Deep Purple. He filled his bedroom with Deep Purple posters, albums, T-shirts and videos.

5 During concerts, he sometimes throws guitar picks into the crowd that are inscribed 'Stolen from Daniel'.

6 He adopted a two-week-old dumped puppy from an animal shelter. You can hear Sweep barking on the song 'Steam Will Rise' on the 'Neon Ballroom' album.

Career highlights

1994: Innocent Criminals win a national demo competition

1995: 'Frogstomp', silverchair's first album, becomes a number one hit in Australia and New Zealand and sells 2.5 million copies throughout the world

1997: 'Freak Show' has three top-ten singles in Australia and goes gold in the US

1999: 'Neon Ballroom' achieves huge sales in Europe and South America. 'Ana's song', about Daniel's battle with anorexia, wins a Comet award

Ned Kelly

Australian folk hero, legend and famous bushranger

Full name: Edward Kelly

Born: December 1854 in Beveridge, Victoria

Died: 11 November 1880 in Melbourne, Victoria

Websites: www.ironoutlaw.com
              nedonline.imagineering.net.au

Early years

Ned's father, Red, was an Irish ex-convict who had been transported to Australia for stealing two pigs. When Ned was twelve his father died. He left school and became 'the man' of the family, helping to look after his seven brothers and sisters. The Kellys moved to a slab hut near Greta, in north-eastern Victoria, to be closer to his mother's family.

A bad lot

Times were tough, and Ned and his mates began to steal horses and cattle from wealthy landowners to get by. His family earned a reputation for being a 'bad lot', and were often picked on by the police whether they'd done anything or not. When he was fifteen, Ned was jailed for six months for being rude to a travelling sales-man's wife. The next year, a mix-up over a stolen horse saw him spend another three years in the lock-up.

An outlaw is born

In 1878, Ned and his brother Dan became 'outlaws' after a fight broke out between a police officer and his family. Constable Fitzpatrick had come to the house to arrest Dan for horse-stealing. After all these years, no one knows what really happened next. According to the Kelly version, Fitzpatrick had been drinking, and made a pass at Ned's fifteen-year-old sister, Kate. When Dan tried to stop him, the police officer's gun went off, and he cut his wrist on the door-latch. However, in his report Fitzpatrick said that Ned had shot him in the wrist. Ned, Dan and their mother Ellen were all charged with attempted murder. Ellen was jailed for three years with her newborn baby, Grace.

The notorious Kelly gang

Ned was furious. He and his brother Dan hooked up with two mates, Steve Hart and Joe Byrne. They became known as the Kelly gang, and spent many months on the run from the police. In October 1878, Ned shot and killed three police officers at Stringybark Creek in the rugged Victorian bush. He spent the next two years robbing banks, taking hostages and dodging police. He left letters behind outlining his fight for justice for the poor, including the famous 'Jerilderie letter'. As he only ever stole from the rich, many people believed in his cause and supported him when he was in trouble.

Ned's last stand

In 1880, a train-load of police arrived in the town of Glenrowan to try to capture the Kelly gang. Ned and his mates were waiting for them on the hotel veranda, dressed in bullet-proof armour made from farm ploughs. The police aimed at Ned's arms and feet, wounding him twenty-eight times, then set fire to the hotel. Ned was the only survivor of his original gang. He was found guilty of murder and sentenced to death. Two weeks later, he was hanged at the Melbourne Gaol, aged twenty-five. Some say his last words were 'Such is life'.

Three interesting things about Ned Kelly

1 He was wearing a green sash underneath his armour the day he was killed. It had been presented to him years before for risking his life to save a drowning boy.

2 The day after Ned was hanged, his head was cut off and his brain taken out and examined by medical students. The rest of his body was buried near the wall of the Old Melbourne Gaol.

3 Queen Victoria declared him the only member of the British Empire that 'anyone' was allowed to kill without getting into trouble.

Ned's criminal record

October 1869: charged with robbing and assaulting a visitor to his property. Released after ten days in jail when the charge was dismissed due to lack of evidence

May 1870: arrested on two charges of highway robbery. Released after six weeks in jail due to lack of evidence

November 1870: charged with assault and insulting a woman. Sentenced to six months jail

August 1871: charged with receiving a stolen horse. Sentenced to three years jail with hard labour

October 1878: declared an outlaw by the Victorian government

October 1880: found guilty of murder and sentenced to death by hanging

☞ Guess what?

The reward for the capture of Ned Kelly and his gang was 8,000 pounds. Today, that amount would be worth about 2 million dollars.

Nicole Kidman

An internationally famous actor

Also known as: Nic

Born: 20 June 1967 in Honolulu, Hawaii

American born

Although her parents are Australian, Nicole was actually born in Honolulu, giving her dual Australian/American citizenship, which was to become very important later in life. The Kidman family lived in Honolulu for a year while Nicole's father was a research student in biochemistry at the University of Hawaii. The following year, the family moved to Washington for three years, before returning home to Sydney.

Drama school

Nicole's parents always encouraged her and her sister Antonia to express themselves and to learn as much as they could about life. Nicole was a confident, strong-willed and rebellious child from the start. She began ballet lessons when she was three, and later learned to play the violin, clarinet and piano. Nicole also loved writing stories. She enrolled in drama school at Sydney's Phillip Street Theatre when she was ten.

Nicole loved the theatre because it allowed her to escape from the constant teasing she received over her height (boys used to call her 'the stork'), pale skin, red hair and freckles. Instead of going to the beach with the other kids, she spent her weekends taking acting or mime classes or working backstage in the gloomy theatre.

From stage to screen

By her mid-teens, Nicole's long legs and 'different' look had become a plus, gaining her heaps of modelling work. Acting, however, was what she really wanted to do. She got her chance at sixteen when she was cast in two Australian movies and a TV series in the same year – *Bush Christmas, BMX Bandits* and an episode of 'Winners'. She dropped out of school to take on more acting work, including the mini-series 'Five Mile Creek', and what is considered to be her breakthrough role – the part of an anti-war protester in the mini-series 'Vietnam'. Then it was off to America to star in the thriller *Dead Calm*, with Sam Neill.

☞ Guess what?

In her first performance, the Lane Cove primary school Nativity play, Nicole dressed up as a sheep in a woolly car-seat cover. She upstaged Mary and the baby Jesus by bleating loudly throughout the performance.

Walk of Fame

Nicole met her husband-to-be Tom Cruise on the set of her next movie, a racetrack romance called *Days* of *Thunder*. Their marriage lasted eleven years before they divorced in 2001. Nicole's breakthrough into the American market didn't come, however, until 1995, when she won several awards for her performance as a fame-crazed housewife turned TV reporter in *To Die For*. Other standout performances include roles in the drama *Eyes Wide Shut*, the spooky ghost movie *The Others*, the sparkling musical *Moulin Rouge*, and her Oscar-winning portrayal of a long-nosed Virginia Woolf in *The Hours*. Nicole firmly cemented her place in movie history in early 2003 by being honoured with a star on Hollywood Boulevard's Walk of Fame.

Seven interesting things about Nicole Kidman

1   When her mother refused to buy her a Barbie doll because she thought it was a sexist toy, Nicole went shopping and bought one for herself.

2   She once tried to turn one of her teachers into a donkey by wiggling her nose like Samantha in the TV show 'Bewitched'.

3   Her parents encouraged Nicole and her sister Antonia to discuss politics or current

affairs at the dinner table, and to hand out 'how-to-vote' cards at election polling booths.

4 She is afraid of butterflies.

5 She had to hide in an open grave with a rat when she was making her second movie, *BMX Bandits*.

6 When she was seventeen she formed a trio with two girlfriends called *Divine Madness*, and sang hit songs at a Sydney pub.

7 She broke a rib while rehearsing a dance routine for the movie *Moulin Rouge*.

Ten movies starring Nicole Kidman

Bush Christmas (1983)

Dead Calm (1989)

Days of Thunder (1990)

Flirting (1991)

Batman Forever (1995)

To Die For (1995)

Eyes Wide Shut (1999)

Moulin Rouge (2001)

The Others (2001)

The Hours (2002)

Charles Kingsford Smith

A flying ace

Full name: Charles Edward Kingsford Smith

Also known as: Smithy, Chilla

Born: 9 February 1897 at Hamilton, Queensland

Died: 7 or 8 November 1935, over the Bay of Bengal

Banknote: $20 (from 1966 to 1993)

Early years

Charles Smith was born in Brisbane at the end of the nineteenth century. When he was five, his family moved to Canada where his dad had a job with the railways. There were seven other families called Smith living in their street, so to help out the postie, they added Kingsford – Charles' mum's surname before her marriage – to their name. When Charles was ten, they returned to Australia, settling in Sydney. Charles loved sport and adventure, and would do anything for a dare.

Flying ace

When world war broke out in 1914, Charles was desperate to join up, but had to wait until he turned eighteen. After basic training he was sent to Egypt, then Gallipoli. He enjoyed tearing around on motorbikes as a dispatch rider, but it was his time in the Royal Flying Corps that gave him a taste for what was to become his passion in life – flying. Now known as 'Smithy', he was soon performing daring stunts, outrunning enemy fire in planes made out of wood and fabric, held together with piano wire.

Smithy's dream

At first, Smithy found it hard to find flying jobs after the war, and took on stunt and charter work for a while. In 1921, he became one of Western Australian Airways' first pilots. His dream, however, was to be the first person to fly across the Pacific Ocean. He raised enough funds to get to America, where he bought a plane he named the *Southern Cross*. In 1928, Smithy, co-pilot Charles Ulm, and two others set off from San Francisco in a tiny plane with an open cockpit. Eighty-three flying hours later, they were met by a huge crowd in Brisbane.

Last flight

Over the next seven years, Smithy continued to set new records for flying, crossing the Atlantic, circling the globe, and flying solo for 16,000 kilometres to take out the England-to-Australia air race. In November 1935 Smithy set out from England on what was to be his last journey. His plane – the *Lady Southern Cross* – crashed somewhere over the Bay of Bengal, near Burma. Although parts of the plane were found, Smithy was never seen again.

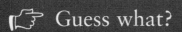

☞ Guess what?

You can see Smithy's plane, the **Southern Cross**, at Brisbane airport.

127

Six interesting things about Charles Kingsford Smith

1 When he was ten, Charlie and two of his friends were pulled from the surf in the first rescue ever performed by Bondi Life Saving Club.

2 During World War I, he survived an attack from two German fighter pilots, who pumped his plane with over 150 bullets. His left foot was hit but he managed to land safely before passing out from loss of blood. Later, three of his toes were amputated.

3 After the war, he and two other fighter pilots set up a joy-riding business. However, the business failed. Their tricky flying skills were a bit too adventurous for most people.

4 In 1920, he worked for Hollywood film studios as a flying stuntman. For one movie, he had to climb out onto the wing and dangle upside down from the struts. He gave movie work away when another stunt pilot flying beside him died when his plane crashed and exploded on impact.

5 He could drink beer standing on his head.

6 When he pulled out of a race because his

plane wasn't ready, people sent him white
feathers through the mail, because they
thought he was a coward.

Career highlights

1917:   receives Military Cross for outstanding
        bravery during World War I

1927:   flies around Australia in record time
        (10 days, 5.5 hours)

1928:   becomes first person to: fly from the USA
        to Australia; fly non-stop across Australia;
        fly from Australia to New Zealand

1930:   becomes first person to complete a
        round-the-world flight

1932:   receives a knighthood

1934:   becomes first person to fly from Australia
        to America across the Pacific Ocean

Wally Lewis

One of Australia's greatest rugby
league players

Full name: Walter James Lewis

Also known as: The King, King Wally

Born: 1 December 1959 in Brisbane, Queensland

Position: five-eighth

Website: www.rleague.com/interactive/trivia

Early years

Wally was born in Brisbane in 1959, and began to play rugby union while at Brisbane State High. An outstanding flyhalf, he was picked to play in the Australian Schoolboys Rugby Union side which toured Europe, Britain and Japan in 1976 and 1977. Another player in the team, Michael O'Connor, went on to become one of Wally's greatest rivals in inter-state competition.

From union to league

At the end of the tour, Wally switched from rugby union to league, moving straight into senior competition. Rugby union was an amateur sport in those days, and players weren't paid. His first games were with Brisbane club, Valleys. In 1984, he switched to Wynnum-Manly, and played there until the Brisbane Broncos came into the New South Wales Rugby League in 1988.

State of Origin

In 1980, Wally was chosen to play at lock forward position for the first ever State of Origin game, against New South Wales. Over the next ten years he played as Queensland five-eighth and captain for thirty out of the thirty-two State of Origin games,

rugby league • football • coaching

more than any other player. With his brilliant long passes and accurate kicking, he picked up a record eight Man of the Match awards, and helped Queensland to become the undisputed Origin match champions.

Test career

Wally played in his first Test for Australia, against France, in 1981, notching up thirty-two more over the next ten years. He became Australian captain in 1984, and held onto this role for the next five seasons, finishing with the 1989 Australian tour of New Zealand. It was during this match that he made one of the greatest tackles of all time.

Four interesting things about Wally Lewis

1 During the 1988 World Cup final against New Zealand, he ordered his team to stand in a semi-circle with their backs to the Kiwis, so the Aussies wouldn't be put off when the Kiwis performed the Maori haka. He also directed his players to fall over when tackled, then move off quickly, so the Kiwis couldn't knock them out of play.

2 He broke his arm during the same match, but kept playing for twenty minutes to make sure Australia was in a good enough position to win the game before he left the field.

3 In Year 12, he spat on a boy who made rude remarks about a girl in his class.

4 He has a reputation for being a hot head. He was once slammed by the media for urging a football crowd to behave badly when they pelted beer cans onto the field after he argued with the referee.

Final years

1990 was a bad year for Wally. He was sacked as captain of the Broncos, and missed the first State of Origin game due to injury.

At the end of the season, after what some people claimed to be a plot against him, he left the Broncos to become captain-coach of the Gold Coast Seagulls. He played his last game in 1992, then took over as coach for Queensland in 1994 for two seasons before bowing out.

These days he works as a television sports commentator.

133

Wally Lewis superstats

Brisbane Broncos: 1988–90
Games: 46 (Tries: 20, Goals: 11, Points: 102)
Gold Coast Seagulls: 1991–92
Games: 34 (Tries: 6, Goals: 3, Points: 30)
Queensland State of Origin Record: 1980–91
Games: 31 (Tries: 7, Goals: 1, F-Goals: 2,
    Points: 30)
Australian International Record: 1981–89, 1991
Tests: 33, Tries: 11, F-Goals: 2, Points: 45)
Captaincies
Queensland captain for his final 30 Origin games
Australian Test captain from 1984–89
Australian captain for 1988 Bicentennial
    International against the Rest-of-the-World
World Cup Championships: 1 (1988, captain)
Kangaroo tours: 2 (captain, 1986)
New Zealand tours: 2 (captain, 1985 and 1989)

☞ Guess what?

In 1985, Wally was awarded the Adidas Golden Boot award for being the finest player in the world.

Norman Lindsay

An exceptionally creative writer
and artist

Full name: Norman Alfred William Lindsay

Born: 22 February 1879 in Creswick, Victoria

Died: 21 November 1969 in Springfield,
New South Wales

Website: www.hermes.net.au/nlg

Early years

Norman Lindsay grew up in a goldfields town in Victoria in the late nineteenth century. He was the fifth child out of a family of six boys and four girls. They all loved dressing up and acting in plays about ancient times. Norman loved drawing and writing stories about the heroes of Greek literature.

His career begins

Norman left home at sixteen and moved to Melbourne to live with his older brother, Lionel. By now a talented artist, he found work as an illustrator for several newspapers and magazines. In 1901 he moved to Sydney, where he was soon creating outrageous political cartoons for the *Bulletin*. He also began to create pen-and-ink sketches, etchings, and watercolour and oil paintings. After two years in London, working for *Punch* magazine, he moved to a stone house at Springwood, in the Blue Mountains. He lived and worked there for more than fifty years. The gardens at Springwood are still full of statues he sculpted himself.

Rudie nudies

Norman's paintings and drawings caused quite a stir, because they were often of nude women. He employed several women to model naked for him, including Rose Soady, who became his second wife. When an art magazine published some of his nudes, its publishers were prosecuted by the police for immorality. One of his novels, *Redheap*, was banned, because the censors thought it was too racy. After a full life, Norman died in 1969, aged ninety.

☞ Guess what?

Norman Lindsay's stone cottage at Springwood, New South Wales, has been set up as a gallery and museum. On display are some of his watercolours, sculptures, ship models and novels, and marionettes from **The Magic Pudding**. Many of his other paintings, etchings and drawings can be seen in galleries around Australia.

The Magic Pudding

In 1918, Norman wrote and illustrated his famous children's book, *The Magic Pudding*. Although fairy stories were popular at the time, he figured what kids were really interested in was stuffing their stomachs with food. So he invented a funny rhyming story about a pudding called Albert. Like the magic packet of Tim Tams on the ad, Albert can renew himself when a slice is cut from him – only in different flavours! In the story, Bunyip Bluegum (a koala), Sam Sawnoff (a penguin) and Bill Barnacle (a sailor) help to keep Albert safe from the terrible Puddin' Thieves, Possum and Wombat. Even though it was written more than eighty years ago, *The Magic Pudding*'s adventures are still popular with kids today.

Four interesting things about Norman Lindsay

1 Four of his nine brothers and sisters, Daryl, Lionel, Percy and Ruby, were artists and/or writers, and so was his son, Jack.

2 He loved making models of ships, and built them exactly to scale.

3 He called the last painting that he did, 'Last Painting'.

4 Elle MacPherson, Kate Fischer and Portia de Rossi frolicked naked around the gardens of Springwood when they appeared as artist's models in the movie based on his life, *Sirens*.

Nine creations by Norman Lindsay

1912: draws 'The Crucified Venus' (featured in the movie, *Sirens*)

1912: completes a model of Captain Cook's ship, the *Endeavour*

1913: writes *Curate in Bohemia*

1918: writes and illustrates *The Magic Pudding*

1918: art magazine *Art in Australia* publishes *The Pen Drawings of Norman Lindsay*

1919: creates first outdoor sculptures

1930: writes *Redheap* (which was banned for the next twenty-nine years on moral grounds)

1931: *Art in Australia* publishes his nude drawings (and is prosecuted by the police)

1970: his autobiography, *My Mask*, is published the year after his death

Eddie Mabo

An Aboriginal activist who gained land rights for his people

Full name: Edward Koiki Mabo

Born: 29 June 1936 on Mer (Murray Island), Torres Strait

Died: 21 January 1992 in Brisbane, Queensland

Early years

Eddie Mabo was born Edward Koiki Sambo on the island of Mer (also known as Murray Island) in Torres Strait. When his mother died shortly after his birth, in accordance with customary law he was given to his mother's brother, Benny Mabo, and his wife to bring up. He was taught all about the land that belonged to his family, as generations of Islanders had been before him. However, at that time, the islands had been taken over by the Queensland government. His people were forced to live on reserves, and existed on government handouts.

Social-justice campaigner

When Eddie was seventeen he got into trouble over a teenage prank, and the Island Council exiled him from Mer. He moved to Townsville and worked in the cane fields and on the railways. During the 1960s he became interested in social justice and the rights of workers. He joined the union movement and became the spokesperson for the Aboriginal and Torres Strait Islander Advancement League. The changes he fought for gave Indigenous people the right to vote and to be counted in the national census. Through his work with the Council for the Rights of Indigenous People (CRIP) he helped to get legal, medical, employment and housing services for his people.

141

The turning point

While working as a gardener at James Cook University, Eddie met Henry Reynolds, a historian who wrote from the point of view of the Aboriginal people. Through discussions with Reynolds, Eddie came to realise that, although he had always thought that his island home belonged to his people, under Australian law it was actually Crown land, owned by the government. Outraged, he vowed to do something about it.

A decade of struggle

Henry Reynolds helped to convince Eddie to present a land rights claim to the High Court of Australia. Eddie and a group of Mer Islanders argued that they were the traditional owners of their lands, on the grounds that they could prove ownership over thirty generations. After ten years of struggle, the High Court finally handed down their decision in favour of the Islanders. But it was too late for Eddie. He had died of cancer six months earlier.

What the Mabo decision means

In 1992, the High Court handed down a decision recognising that the Aboriginal peoples of Australia had a right to 'possession, occupation, use and enjoyment' of their ancestral lands. In other words, it was their land, and they had the right to do whatever they wanted with it. The court rejected what is known as the **terra nullius** (no one's land) view — which is that no one actually owned the land when the British arrived in 1788, so it was okay for them to claim it. The decision meant that other Indigenous groups could now put forward their own cases for land rights or compensation for its loss. However, new legislation since then has meant that, so far, no other land claims have been successful.

Three interesting things about Eddie Mabo

1 He and his wife, Bonita Neehow, raised ten children.

2 In 1972, when his father was suffering from tuberculosis, Eddie and his family were

refused permission by the Queensland government to return to Mer to visit him. Eddie was told that, because he had not lived on Mer for a long time, he was no longer considered to be an Islander. Six weeks later, his father died.

3 When Eddie's grave in Townsville was vandalised, his family took his body back home to Mer. The Islanders performed a traditional ceremony of the kind normally reserved for kings.

Career highlights

1962: becomes secretary of the Aboriginal and Torres Strait Islander Advancement League

1970: elected president of CRIP

1973: appointed director of the Black Community School, Townsville, which helped preserve Indigenous culture

1992: High Court of Australia supports the land rights claim; named Australian of the Year; awarded a Human Rights Medal

Mary MacKillop

A Catholic nun who is likely to become Australia's first saint

Full name: Maria Ellen MacKillop

Born: 15 January 1842 in Fitzroy, Victoria

Died: 8 August 1909 in Sydney, New South Wales

Personal motto: Never see an evil without trying to find a remedy.

Early years

Mary MacKillop was the eldest of eight children, and her family was very poor. They were evicted from their house in Melbourne several times, and often had to depend on relatives for help. Because her father was often away from home, Mary spent a lot of her time looking after her younger brothers and sisters. She also paid all the family's bills by working as a governess and store clerk while she was still a teenager.

From Penola to Portland

When Mary turned eighteen, she went to Penola, in South Australia, to work as a governess for her aunt's ten children. She was a very religious girl, and when she saw that many kids in the area were too poor to go to school, she began to dream about starting up her own schools in remote areas for children from poor families. After two years with her aunt, she moved to another set of relations in Portland, western Victoria. This time, she was in charge of fourteen kids, for very little pay. She was relieved when she was offered the job as a teacher at the local Catholic school.

Doing God's work

After a scandal at the school, where Mary was unfairly asked to leave, she returned to Penola. Although she loved teaching, she was also keen to follow a religious life, and become a nun. The parish priest, Father Woods, helped her to set up a school in a converted stable. In 1866, Mary became the first member of the Sisters of St Joseph. Soon, other women joined her. In the following years, they set up new schools and orphanages, as well as hostels for unmarried mothers and refuges for the aged, all over the country. Although Mary lived a poor and humble life herself, she was happy, because she believed she was finally doing the work God wanted her to do.

☞ Guess what?

The canonisation process – which people have to go through before they can become saints – is often very slow. So far, Mary's has taken more than seventy-five years. However, this is nothing compared to Joan of Arc's – which took 500 years, and Albert of Cologne's – 650!

Excommunication

Mary's independence annoyed Church leaders, and she was thrown out of the Church by the Bishop of Adelaide after an argument about who should rule her order of nuns. The next year, just before he died, he changed his mind, and Mary and her followers were accepted back. She then went to Rome to have her Order approved by the Pope, so that other bishops wouldn't try something similar. Over the next thirty years, St Joseph's schools were opened all over Australia and New Zealand.

The road to sainthood

Mary died in 1909. Over the course of her life she had inspired 600 others to join her in helping more than 12,000 children. In 1926, people began the long process to have her declared a saint. In 1995, after her followers provided proof of her performing a miracle, she was declared to be 'Blessed' by Pope John Paul II. Now the world is waiting for proof of her second miracle.

Steps to becoming a saint

1 Prove that you're suitable and have all the right qualities by passing an examination (a bit like a court trial) where witnesses argue your case.

2 Get someone to write a report on your life and goodness then argue your case before the cardinals in Rome.

3 Perform a documented miracle. In Mary's case, her spirit is believed to have answered the prayers of someone who was dying of leukaemia. (This will guarantee you sainthood in your own country, but not around the world. To gain this you must fulfil Step 4.)

4 Perform a second miracle.

Career highlights

1866:   becomes the first member of the Sisters of Saint Joseph in Penola

1867:   opens her first school in Adelaide

1873:   gains approval from Pope Pius IX to set up The Order of the Sisters of Saint Joseph

1926:   the process to have her declared a saint begins

1995:   named 'Blessed Mary MacKillop' by Pope John Paul

Jesse Martin

The youngest person to sail non-stop
around the world on his own

Born: 26 August 1981 near Munich, Germany

Websites: www.jessemartin.net; www.kijana.net

Early years

Jesse was born in a German village – his parents had been travelling around Europe in a kombi van. When he was five weeks old, his family returned to Australia. They lived for a while in Upwey, then moved to a home-made cabin in the Daintree area of far-north Queensland. Jesse lived a 'Jungle Boy' life-style, fishing and snorkelling on the reef, and running through the rainforest. His parents encouraged him to believe he could go anywhere and do anything.

☞ Guess what?

Jesse's equipment list on the **Lionheart** included one pair of shoes (skate shoes), more than sixty CDs, and a hundred books, and $7,400 worth of freeze-dried or long-life food. His satellite phone bills averaged between $2,500 and $3,000 per month.

First trip

When he was in Year 8, Jesse and his twelve-year-old brother Beau were taught to sail by their dad, Kon. They then took off on a 1000-kilometre trip, sailing from Cairns to Cape York on a 3-metre long catamaran.

While they were travelling they called in at Lizard Island, a tropical resort which attracted luxury yachts to its bays. Jesse figured sailing one of those yachts had to be a more comfortable way to travel than floating around on an open catamaran, covered in salt. He spent the rest of the trip dreaming about fitting out his own yacht and sailing it around the world.

Getting ready

Jesse decided he wanted to be the youngest person to sail unassisted non-stop around the world. To get ready for his trip, he started taking sailing lessons and finding out about the things he'd need to know onboard: everything from navigation to meteorology and first aid. He sent off seventy-five letters to companies, asking them to sponsor his trip. None of them was interested in sponsoring a fifteen-year-old. Rather than totally give up his dream, he decided to join the crew on someone else's boat instead. After a couple of false starts, he sailed from Belize (near Mexico), through the Panama Canal and across the Pacific Ocean to Tahiti.

Living the dream

Finally, with the help of his mother and several sponsors, Jesse bought and fitted out a second-hand

10-metre yacht, named *Lionheart*. Ignoring criticism from people who told him he was too young, and the trip too unsafe, he finally set sail on 7 December 1998, three months after his seventeenth birthday. During the 328 days he spent alone at sea, he faced many sticky situations, including gale-force winds, towering waves, icebergs and inquisitive whales. There were also long periods where everything was quiet and he was incredibly lonely. To fill in time, he listened to music, read books, played his guitar, answered kids' emails, talked to friends by satellite phone and wrote a weekly news column. On 31 August 1999, 25,000 people turned up to the beach at Sandringham to cheer him home.

What Jesse did next

On his return, Jesse was showered with awards recognising his spirit and determination to succeed, including Young Victorian of the Year, and Australian Youth Sailor of the Year. He also spent time working with several youth organisations, inspiring other young people to believe in themselves and their own abilities. In March 2002, together with a group of friends, he set out on a two-year land-and-sea voyage in an old-style wooden yacht, the *Kijana*. However, various problems caused him to leave the boat in February 2003.

Amazing facts about Jesse's solo journey

1 He sailed 27,000 nautical miles (50,000 kilometres) in just under 11 months.

2 No fossil fuels were used on the journey. His boat was powered by wind, and any electricity needed on board came from the sun and wind through the use of solar panels and a wind generator.

3 He used only half a bottle of shampoo on the trip, and, because he forgot to pack a comb, combed his hair with a fork.

4 The *Lionheart* suffered five knockdowns in one night, when it was hit by huge waves. Whenever this happened, everything in the cabin got soaking wet.

5 He threw out all his wet weather gear by mistake, thinking it was rubbish.

Douglas Mawson

A scientist and Antarctic explorer and one of the first Australians to reach the South Magnetic Pole

Born: 5 May 1882 in Shipley, England

Died: 14 October 1958 in Adelaide, South Australia

Website: www.mawson.sa.gov.au

Banknote: $100 (from 1984 to 1996)

Early years

Originally from England, Douglas's family emigrated to Australia when he was two. They settled in Rooty Hill, near Sydney. Douglas was always fascinated by nature and spent hours studying rocks and wondering about how the Earth had been formed. He was a brilliant student, and began studying geology and engineering at Sydney University when he was only sixteen.

Glaciers and rocks

After he graduated, Douglas became a lecturer at the University of Adelaide. He took students to the Flinders Ranges to study the rocks, which had been sculpted by glaciers millions of years ago. He started wondering about Antarctica, where glaciers could still be found. Explorers from all around were just starting to unlock the secrets of its frozen wastes, and he longed to join them. In 1907, he got his chance when he joined an expedition to Antarctica, led by British explorer Ernest Shackleton.

Twin tasks

Douglas and another Australian, Professor Edgeworth David, were given two tasks on the expedition. One was to climb nearly 4,000 metres to the top of Mount

Erebus, an active volcano, where they found a crater bubbling with red-hot lava, surrounded by sparkling snow. They saved time on the way back by sliding down the sides of the mountain. The other task was to find the South Magnetic Pole. This is the place where both hands of the compass become vertical. They walked for four months, dragging their supply-laden sled over 2,000 kilometres of frozen land.

Australasian Antarctic Expedition

In 1911, Douglas returned to Antarctica, this time as the leader of an Australasian expedition. He wanted to explore and map the coastal area of Antarctica closest to Australia. Five research groups set out on foot to explore different regions. Douglas Mawson, Lieutenant Belgrave Ninnis and Dr Xavier Mertz headed east with a team of huskies. The conditions were terrible, with roaring winds, slippery ice and poor light.

Disaster falls

Five weeks after the journey began, Belgrave hurtled into a crevasse, taking his dog team and most of the food with him. He was never seen again. Douglas and Dr Mertz began the long journey back, but were soon forced to shoot and eat the remaining dogs. When Dr Mertz became sick and died from the poison in the dogs' livers, Douglas cut his sled in half and struggled on alone. His hair fell out and the skin on the soles of his feet died and fell off. After an incredible ordeal, during which he hauled himself out of a crevasse with a rope, he finally made it back to base camp.

Future research

In 1929 and 1931, Douglas led two more expeditions to the Antarctic, claiming forty-two per cent of the vast continent as Australian Territory. His studies of marine biology and oceanography helped form the basis of later Antarctic research. He died of a stroke in 1958, aged seventy-six.

Three interesting things about Douglas Mawson

1 When his family were sailing out to Australia on the *Ellora*, two-year-old Douglas kept trying to climb up the masts of the ship. The crew rescued him each time.

2 When he was at school, his headmaster was convinced he would become an explorer. He told people that if there was any place left in the world to explore, Douglas would be the one to lead an expedition to it.

3 The first thing the members of the Australian expedition did when they arrived in Antarctica in 1911 was to build a hut to keep them safe from the 300-kilometre-per-hour winds which threatened to blow them off their feet. They called their hut 'Home of the Blizzard'.

Career highlights

1907:   joins Sir Ernest Shackleton's expedition

1908:   climbs Mount Erebus, an active volcano

1909:   becomes the first person to locate the South Magnetic Pole

1911:   begins the Australasian Antarctic Expedition

1914:   receives a knighthood, the King's Polar Medal, and the Royal Geographical Society's Founder's Medal

1929:   leads an expedition of British, Australian and New Zealand explorers to Antarctica

☞ Guess what?

Australia's first permanent Antarctic Base, Mawson Station, was set up in 1954.

Nellie Melba

An opera singer who became Australia's first international star

Full name: Helen Porter Mitchell

Also known as: The Queen of Song

Born: 19 May 1861 in Richmond, Victoria

Died: 23 February 1931 in Sydney, New South Wales

Banknote: $100

Early years

Nellie Mitchell's mum and dad were both musical, and there was always lots of music in the house. Nellie's mum, Isabella, was her first music teacher. By the time Nellie was twelve she was the organist at Scots Church in the city, which her father had built. One day, her dad told her that if she learnt to play twelve pieces of music by heart, he'd give her a gold watch. She did, and he kept his promise. Her musical career had begun.

Opera lessons

By the time she'd finished school, Nellie was sure she wanted to be a singer. She began to take lessons from a retired Italian opera singer, Pietro Cecchi. When she was twenty, both her mother and her little sister Vere died. Her father took up a new job and moved his family to Queensland. Here Nellie met and married a charming young man named Charlie Armstrong, and they had a son, George. However, she soon grew tired of life in a rain-soaked cottage, and moved back to Melbourne to pursue her singing career, while her sisters took care of the baby.

From Mitchell to Melba

In 1884, when she was twenty-two, Nellie wowed the audiences in her first professional appearance at the

Melbourne Town Hall. Two years later, she hit the concert stages of London, but without much success. It was only after a year of hard work with Madame Mathilde Marchesi, a famous singing teacher in Paris, that Nellie came into her own. Madame wanted her to have a more memorable and European-sounding name, so she changed her surname from Mitchell to Melba, using the first part of her home town, Melbourne.

> ## ☞ Guess what?
>
> In 1893, George Escoffier, a famous French chef, created a dessert in honour of Nellie Melba. Called Peach Melba, it's made with poached peaches and vanilla ice-cream, drizzled with raspberry sauce.

The Queen of Song

After a brilliant debut in Brussels, Melba took the rest of Europe by storm. She was soon considered to be one of the most talented and famous opera singers of all time. People began calling her the 'Queen of Song'. In 1902, she toured around Australia and New Zealand, often to tiny towns. Audiences treated her like a superstar, climbing onto the roof or crawling under the stage of the hall to catch the sound of her voice. For the next few years, she divided her time between Australia and Europe, gaining new fans wherever she went.

Final farewell

Nellie kept singing well into her sixties. Although she announced her retirement from the stage in 1926, she kept giving 'farewell' performances for another three years. She died of a blood infection in 1931, aged sixty-nine.

Five interesting things about Nellie Melba

1. Nellie hated being carted off to church by her parents every Sunday. She'd arrange to get mud all over her good clothes so she could stay behind.

2. To shield herself from the icy water of the 6.00 a.m. shower she had to take every day at boarding school, Nellie took an umbrella into the shower stall with her.

3. She was one of the first opera singers to have her voice recorded. Between 1904 and 1926, she made nearly 200 records.

4 She thought that, as the *prima donna* (lead singer) in the opera house, she should get the most attention. Once, she stopped flowers from being delivered to the stage for a co-star because she thought *she* should be the only one to get flowers.

5 Nellie gave so many 'farewell' concerts, she inspired a saying that people still use today when they find it hard to leave somewhere without saying goodbye to everyone: 'More farewells than Nellie Melba'.

Career highlights

1884: first professional performance at Melbourne Town Hall

1887: operatic debut in Brussels

1902: concert tour of Australia and New Zealand

1909: begins 16,000 kilometre tour of Australia

1918: becomes Dame of the British Empire (DBE)

1926: final British performance, at Covent Garden, London

1927: performance at the opening of Parliament House in Canberra

1928: final Australian performance, at Geelong, Victoria

Robert Menzies

Australia's longest serving Prime Minister

Full name: Robert Gordon Menzies

Also known as: Ming, Pig-Iron Bob

Born: 20 December 1894 in Jeparit, Victoria

Died: 15 May 1978 in Melbourne, Victoria

Early years

Robert was born in the back room of his dad's grocery store in Jeparit, a Victorian country town, in 1894. As a child, Robert loved talking, and seemed to have an opinion on everything. When he was twelve, he went to live with his grandparents in Ballarat. He was a good student, topping the State exams when he was thirteen, and winning several scholarships and prizes. In 1916, he graduated from Melbourne University with first-class honours in Law.

From law to politics

After a dazzling ten-year career as a lawyer, Robert switched to politics. He started out as a member of the Victorian Parliament, then switched to Federal politics, winning a seat in the House of Representatives in 1934. He was a brilliant speaker, good at entertaining and informing his audiences. However, he was never very popular. Many people thought he was arrogant, talking down to anyone he didn't think was as good as himself.

In and out

When Prime Minister Joseph Lyons suddenly died in 1939, Robert took over his job. He never had the full support of his party, however, and two years later he resigned. It looked like his political career was over. However, instead of totally throwing in the towel, he spent some time thinking about the mistakes he'd made, and came up with the plan for a new political party – the Liberals.

A new party

The Liberal Party would look out for ordinary tax-payers, or the 'forgotten people', as Robert called them. He vowed to represent the type of people who wanted a quiet life, living in their own home and working in a secure job. He counted on their fear of the country being invaded and overtaken by communists – the 'red scare' – and used this to help him win the 1949 Federal Election. Robert Menzies was back in power.

A long career

By now known as Bob, Robert went on to become Australia's longest serving Prime Minister, staying in power for sixteen years. During this time, he made many reforms in areas such as immigration, education and research, and helped to make the country a better place to live for most people, with plenty of jobs and cheap housing. However not everyone agreed with his policies. There was public outcry when he introduced compulsory National Service, sending many twenty-year-olds into the army against their will. His decision to send troops to fight alongside the American soldiers in the Vietnam War was also unpopular. In 1966, realising that times had changed, and that many Australian people were no longer behind him, Bob resigned. He died in 1978.

Three interesting things about Robert Menzies

1 He always believed he would achieve greatness. While he was at university he bragged that he would become either the chief justice or the prime minister.

2 Although his elder brothers enlisted in the army when World War I broke out, Robert decided to stay at home instead. This caused him a lot of trouble in 1965, when he made the unpopular decision to send Australian troops to the Vietnam War.

3 He was the Number One ticket-holder at the Carlton Football Club. During his last years, he used to park his black Bentley limousine so that it overlooked Princes Park (now Optus Oval). Shielded behind tinted windows, he'd watch the match from the privacy of his car.

Career highlights

1928:   elected to the Victorian Parliament

1929:   becomes the youngest ever King's Council (senior barrister)

1934:   wins a by-election and enters Federal Parliament

1939:   becomes Prime Minister

1949:   enters second term as Prime Minister

1963:   knighted by the Queen (Knight of the Thistle)

1976:   appointed Knight of the Order of Australia (AK)

☞ Guess what?

Robert Menzies loved everything to do with England, particularly the Queen. In 1966, when decimal currency replaced the old system of money, he wanted dollars to be called 'royals'. When people laughed at his suggestion, he withdrew it.

Kylie Minogue

One of the most successful
pop stars in the world

Full name: Kylie Ann Minogue

Also known as: The Singing Budgie; Bruiser;
The Princess of Pop

Born: 28 May 1968 in Melbourne, Victoria

Websites: www.kylie.co.uk, www.kylie.com

Early years

Kylie grew up in suburban Melbourne. She and her friends used to dress up in party frocks and mime to Abba records, using broom handles as microphones. When she was ten, she went along to an audition for a small part in a TV show that her younger sister Dannii was hoping to get. When the casting director saw Kylie, he gave her the part instead. Oops. She was soon acting in a second series, 'Skyways', set in an airport. A chubby Jason Donovan played her brother.

Her big break

Over the next four years it was Dannii who became the star, scoring heaps of fan mail as a regular performer on 'Young Talent Time'. Feeling a bit left out in the cold, Kylie answered a newspaper ad looking for young actors to star in a series called 'The Henderson Kids'. She got the part, and impressed the directors so much with her acting ability, she was soon appearing in other shows. But it wasn't until she was seventeen that she got her big break, playing car mechanic Charlene Mitchell in the long-running TV soap, 'Neighbours'.

Number One

While she was making 'Neighbours', Kylie and a few of her friends from the show sang the song 'Locomotion'

singing • dancing • movies

171

at a charity gig. She was invited to record it and soon had a hit single on her hands. But it wasn't until she moved to London that her career really took off, and she was soon popping out a string of Number One hits. Kylie took up with her co-star from 'Neighbours', Jason Donovan, releasing their duet 'Especially For You' in 1988. She also returned to acting, playing the lead in the movie *The Delinquents*.

☞ Guess what?

In 1998, Kylie changed the title of her new album from 'Impossible Princess' to plain old 'Kylie Minogue' because it was thought it would clash with the tragic death of Princess Diana.

Change of style

In 1990, Kylie changed her image from the bubbly 'girl-next-door' to 'raunchy Kylie'. She wore sexier outfits and dated Michael Hutchence, at the time the lead singer of Aussie band INXS. She continued to record with other artists, including Nick Cave and the Bad Seeds and the Manic Street Preachers, and starred as a British spy in the movie *Street Fighter*, with martial arts legend Jean-Claude Van Damme.

From hotpants to thongs

In 2000, Kylie brought hotpants back into fashion when she released the smash hit dance single 'Spinning Around'. Later that year, Kylie arrived on a giant rubber thong to sing two of her songs in front of a TV audience of 4 billion people at the Sydney Olympics closing ceremony. In 2001, Kylie's catchy song 'Can't Get You Out of My Head' not only hit the top of the charts around the world, it cracked the difficult American market, confirming her unofficial title, 'Princess of Pop'.

Six interesting things about Kylie Minogue

1 Her first thirteen releases all reached the Top Ten, and 'Can't Get You out of My Head' was a Number One hit in every country it was released.

2 In 1988, she became the first person ever to win four Logie awards in one night. Other awards to her credit include the Sexiest Person on the Planet and the Coolest Female in Music.

3 The hotpants she wore in the 'Spinning Around' video were picked up for 50 pence (about $1.30) on a market stall.

4 Soon after she became famous, she burnt all her teenage diaries to stop reporters finding out anything about her private life.

5 English newspapers make up lots of gossip and scandal about her. Her favourite headlines include, 'Is Kylie an Alien?'

6 Kylie's wax statue at Madame Tussaud's in London was the most 'touched' of any of the statues in the museum. It became so damaged it was replaced in 1998 by a new-look Kylie wearing a black lace slip.

Nine hit songs for Kylie

'I Should Be So Lucky' (1987)

'Especially for You' (with Jason Donovan) (1988)

'Better the Devil You Know' (1990)

'Shocked' (1991)

'Confide in Me' (1994)

'Where the Wild Roses Grow' (with Nick Cave) (1995)

'Spinning Around' (2000)

'Can't Get You Out of My Head' (2001)

'In Your Eyes' (2002)

LA TROBE PICTURE COLLECTION, STATE LIBRARY OF VICTORIA

Harry 'Breaker' Morant

An Australian soldier who was controversially executed by firing squad during the Boer War

Full name: Harry Harbord Morant
(Edwin Henry Murrant)

Also known as: the Breaker

Born: 9 December 1864 in Bridgewater, England

Died: 27 February 1902 in Pretoria, South Africa

Early years

The details of Harry's birth are rather mysterious. Harry always claimed that he was born in Devon, England in 1865, the son of Admiral Sir George Digby Morant. However, research by historians suggests that he might have made this up. Their view is that he was actually born a year earlier in a workhouse in another part of England, and that his real name had been Edwin Henry Murrant. Another part of the mystery is the identity of his real father. Whoever he was paid for Harry's education at an exclusive boys' boarding school.

A new life in Australia

In 1883, when he was seventeen, Harry left England for a new life in Australia. Once again, there are several differing explanations for the move, which range from being forced to flee England because of bad debts, to a scandal involving a young heiress. Not long after arriving in Queensland, Harry got a job with a travelling circus heading for Charters Towers, south-west of Townsville. A few weeks later, he married Daisy O'Dwyer, a governess in the area, but the marriage didn't last long. Daisy later became famous in her own right (as Daisy Bates) for her work with Aboriginal people.

The Breaker

Over the next fifteen years, Harry travelled around Queensland and New South Wales, working as a drover and horse-breaker. He soon earned the nickname 'the Breaker' for his flashy riding skills and clever way with wild mountain horses. He was also a poet, and several of his ballads about the bush were published in the Sydney *Bulletin*, alongside the poems of Banjo Paterson and Henry Lawson.

The Boer War

In 1899, war broke out in South Africa between the British, who were ruling the country, and the Dutch settlers (known as Boers), who wanted to set up their own Boer republic. British and colonial troops, including volunteer soldiers from Australia, were sent in to crush the rebellion. Harry signed up to fight with the South Australian Mounted Rifles in January 1900, and quickly rose through the ranks. After some time out in England, he re-enlisted in 1901, along with a new friend, Captain Hunt.

The Bushveldt Carbineers

By this time the war was getting nasty, with Dutch armed farmers making guerrilla raids on the British troops. Harry joined a special fighting unit called the

military • writing

Bushveldt Carbineers. They were tough and fearless, and set out to fight the Boers on their own terms. His friend Captain Hunt was killed brutally and sadistically during an ambush that went wrong. When an angry Harry discovered a Boer prisoner wearing his mate's jacket, he shot him, along with several other men and a German missionary who'd been acting suspiciously.

Accused of murder

Seven of the Carbineers, including Harry and another Australian, Peter Handcock, were accused of murdering the prisoners and the missionary. The whole trial was a sham, and they were only given an inexperienced lawyer to defend their case. Harry claimed that it had been okay for him to kill the Boers, because the British commander had personally instructed him to take no prisoners.

However, he was still found guilty. The outcome of the trial caused a huge stir back home, because not only did the British make their decision without consulting the Australian government, but several British soldiers who had also killed prisoners were let off. Harry and Peter were executed by firing squad in 1902.

☞ Guess what?

On 27 February 2001, ninety-nine years to the day after they were executed, a jumbo jet brought Harry's and Peter's bones back to Australia from their graves in South Africa.

Four interesting things about Breaker Morant

1 His marriage broke down when his new wife kicked him out after he failed to pay for their wedding, then got into trouble with the police for stealing some pigs and a saddle.

2 During his home leave from the Boer War, Harry became engaged to two different women.

3 When the Boers staged a surprise attack on the town where his trial was being held, Harry and the other accused men were asked to join in the fight to stave them off. It made no difference to the trial however, and Harry and his mates were still found guilty.

4 Harry's trial has inspired several books, a play and a movie, *Breaker Morant*.

military • writing

Johnny O'Keefe

Australia's first rock'n'roll star

Full name: John Michael O'Keefe

Also known as: The Wild One, J O'K

Born: 19 January 1935 in Dover Heights,
New South Wales

Died: 6 October 1978 in Sydney, New South Wales

Website: www.johnnyokeefe.net

Early years

Johnny O'Keefe's family called him 'Little Devil' because he was always getting into trouble. His mum played piano and his dad had once played in a band called The Club Royals. Johnny learnt to play piano and trumpet, and spent hours glued to the radio, listening to hit songs of the 1940s. By the time he was fourteen he'd put together a vocal trio with two classmates.

The breakthrough

Johnny's breakthrough came not long after he'd left school. When the advertised star failed to turn up for a concert, Johnny convinced the promoter to let him sing instead. He performed the Johnnie Ray song 'Cry', wearing a pair of glasses hooked up to a rubber tube filled with water. Every time he squeezed the tube, water ran down his face. Next, he jumped down off the stage into the audience and held the hand of an old lady while he crooned 'Walking My Baby Back Home' to her. The audience went wild, and Johnny's career was on its way.

Rock'n'roll

In 1955, Johnny went to see the movie *Blackboard Jungle*, which featured the rock'n'roll music of Bill

Haley and the Comets. It changed his life. He put together a band called the Dee Jays and began hanging round the offices of Lee Gordon, a big-name promoter, hoping to get a gig. The Dee Jays were soon doing warm-up acts for big bands. Johnny dressed up in colourful stage gear and gyrated his body around the stage, earning himself the name 'The Wild One'. He began recording hit songs, becoming Australia's first rock'n'roller. It was now the Dee Jays' turn to headline at Lee Gordon's Stadium Shows.

Cars and scars

In 1959, Johnny and his band became the regular act on Australia's first national TV rock program, 'Six O'Clock Rock'. Later, Johnny became compere, helping young local artists such as Olivia Newton John and Peter Allen on their paths to international success. He scored a recording deal with a major American label, Liberty Records, but failed to make it big in the States. In 1960, he fell asleep while returning from a gig, and collided with a gravel truck. Even though Johnny had ninety stitches to his hands and face, and needed extensive plastic surgery, he was soon back on TV, and recording more hit songs. Some people, however, believe he never really recovered from the accident.

Three interesting things about Johnny O'Keefe

1 He was always getting into trouble at school. One time he and a friend sneaked out of class and changed all the route numbers on the school buses. All the bus travellers ended up at the wrong destinations.

2 At his first gigs at the Bondi Auditorium, the audience pelted him with eggs and tomatoes.

3 He banned musicians with long hair from appearing on his TV show 'Sing, Sing, Sing' because it was a 'family' show.

The downside of fame

Johnny's popularity continued to grow and over the next few years he recorded more hit songs and hosted new TV shows. The pressure of fame and work eventually caught up with him, however, and he suffered several breakdowns. By the time 'Beatlemania' hit, Johnny's style of music was on the way out. Never one to give up, he made several comebacks over the next fifteen years, including a wild performance at the Sunbury rock festival in 1973. By the end of the show, he'd converted 35,000 hippies to rock 'n' roll. Johnny died of a heart attack in 1978, aged only forty-three.

Johnny O'Keefe superstats

- 35 Top 40 hits over a 26-year career
- 'I'm Counting on You' spent 10 weeks at Number One in 1961
- First Australian artist to make the Top 40 charts
- First Australian rock artist to get a recording contract
- First Australian rock artist to be signed by a major international label

Six hit songs by Johnny O'Keefe

'Wild One'
'She's My Baby'
'Shout'
'Move Baby Move'
'Save the Last Dance For Me'
'So Tough'

☞ Guess what?

Shout!, a musical based on J O'K's life, with Jimmy Barnes' son David Campbell in the lead role, was first performed in 2001.

Banjo Paterson

One of Australia's favourite bush poets

Full name: Andrew Barton Paterson

Also known as: Barty, Banjo

Born: 17 February 1864 on Narambla Station, New South Wales

Died: 5 February 1941 in Sydney, New South Wales

Banknote: $10

Early years

Andrew Barton Paterson was born on a cattle station near Orange, New South Wales. A few years later, the family moved to Illalong, near the Snowy Mountains. Their property was on the main route between Melbourne and Sydney, and Barty (as he was called) loved watching the drovers, bullock teams and Cobb and Co. coaches passing by. On school days he'd walk up the paddock to catch his pony, then ride 6 kilometres to school.

After school

When he turned ten, Barty was sent off to live with his granny so he could go to school in Sydney. He couldn't wait for the holidays to get back to the bush, and go camping and riding with his five younger brothers and sisters. When he was sixteen he started work as a clerk with a law firm, and later became a lawyer. His first published piece of writing was a political pamphlet arguing that small farmers were getting a raw deal when it came to government land grants.

Love of the bush

By the time he was twenty, Barty had a new interest – writing poetry. He began sending poems about life in the bush to a popular newspaper called the *Bulletin*.

He invented a pen name for himself – 'the Banjo' – which was the name of his family's favourite race horse. Readers of the *Bulletin* loved his poems, especially 'The Man from Snowy River'. At the end of the nineteenth century, people were starting to think of themselves as 'Australian', rather than British. Banjo's poems were full of 'real' Australian characters and settings: stockmen, bullockies, drovers, shearers, bark huts, billabongs and gum trees.

☞ Guess what?

Several movies and TV series based on his poems have been made, and words and scenes from 'The Man from Snowy River' appear on the $10 note.

Waltzing Matilda

In 1895, Banjo's first collection of poetry sold out in a week. He was suddenly a celebrity. However, just like Clancy in 'Clancy of the Overflow', he longed to get out of the city and back to the bush. He travelled north-west to Winton, Queensland, to visit his fiancee, Sarah Riley. While he was there he heard a local legend about a wanted man who had drowned himself rather than be captured by police. He also heard the term 'waltzing Matilda' for the first time. It was how swagmen described the way they carried their bundle of belongings around. He put the two things together and came up with some song lyrics. Friends wrote music for them and bingo – 'Waltzing Matilda' was born. Or so the story goes.

A long career

Banjo continued his career as a writer for many years. He wrote about his travels in northern Australia and became the war correspondent for several papers during the Boer War in South Africa. During World War I he served as an ambulance driver in France, then used his riding experience to help train thousands of horses for the Australian Light Horse Regiment in Egypt. He worked as a newspaper editor and wrote several books before returning to farming in 1930. He was awarded the CBE (Commander of the British Empire) in 1939, and died two years later, aged seventy-seven.

Three interesting things about Banjo Paterson

1 When he was a kid the station rouseabout took him to the picnic races at Bogolong.

The horses were tough mountain ponies ridden by wild horsemen from Snowy River country. One rider borrowed the light saddle from Barty's pony to ride in the main race – and won.

2 His poems were very different from the work of another writer of the time, his rival Henry Lawson. Henry wrote stories and poems about the hardships and heartbreak of bush life, while Banjo's were full of fun and adventure.

3 Many of his poems are based on real places and people. He got the idea for 'The Geebung Polo Club' after playing a polo match against Cooma, where just like in the poem, the men were wild, and wore cabbage-tree hats and skin-tight pants.

Six Poems by Banjo Paterson

The Man from Snowy River
A Bush Christening
The Man from Ironbark
Saltbush Bill
Mulga Bill's Bicycle
The Geebung Polo Club

Gillian Rolton

The first Australian woman to win Olympic
gold in a horse-riding event

Born: 3 May 1956 in Adelaide, South Australia

Website: www.gillian-rolton.com

Early days

Gillian was born in Adelaide in 1956. Desperate for a horse, she kept bugging her parents to buy her one. However, worried that she might hurt herself riding, they refused, even though her older brother had owned a horse, called Starry. Gillian was good at lots of different sports and eventually settled on swimming. She trained hard and made the State squad when she was ten. When her school wouldn't let her take time off to go to the championships, she packed it in. She became so miserable that her parents finally relented and bought her an ex-pacer named Randy.

Saville Row

For the next ten years, Gillian rode in Show and Dressage events, winning the Champion Equestrienne and Champion Lady Rider at the Royal Adelaide Show. When she was twenty-one, she bought a yearling horse for $200. Saville Row was a bit too lively for dressage events, but he loved jumping, so she started to enter Eventing and Showjumping events. They did so well that in 1983, Gillian made the 'long list' for the 1984 Olympic Games in Los Angeles. Unfortunately, Saville Row hurt his leg during the final selection trials, and had to be retired. Gillian, however, was determined to try again.

Third time lucky

When the trials for the 1988 Seoul Olympics came up, Gillian was once again long-listed, with a horse called Benton's Way. This time, however, it was Gillian who was injured, dislocating her elbow in a training accident the day before the trial. In 1992, it was third time lucky. Riding a big grey horse called Peppermint Grove, Gillian made it on to the team for the Three Day Event at the Barcelona Olympics. In this event, four riders compete, but only the top three scores are counted. When David Green's horse was injured during the cross-country section, Gillian suddenly found herself facing heaps of pressure. She came through with a near-perfect score, and the Australian team won its first gold medal since 1960 for that event.

Back-to-back gold

Four years later, Gillian saddled up once again for the 1996 Olympics in Atlanta. She fell twice during the cross-country event, breaking her collarbone and two ribs. However, determined not to let her team down, she got back on the horse after each fall, and completed the course. She then handed the reins to teammate Wendy Schaeffer, who took her place for the show-jumping, even though Wendy had a pin in her leg from a fall two months earlier. Wendy jumped brilliantly, and the Aussie team won another gold for the second year in a row.

Clarendon Park

A year later, Peppermint Grove retired. He lives in comfort at Clarendon Park, a centre Gillian set up to train other talented horses for international events. He keeps in shape by acting as lead pony, taking kids and their horses down to the beach, through the forest or over cross-country fences. Gillian missed out on qualifying for the 2000 Olympics with her next horse Endeavour, but has had lots of success with her new horse Aspire. She is currently working as a National Eventing Selector and International Judge.

Career highlights

1982: wins Australian One Day and Two Day Event Championships

1990: selected to represent Australia at the International Olympic Academy in Greece

1992: South Australian Sportswoman of the Year; SA Institute of Sport Female Athlete of the Year

1993: awarded Order of Australia Medal for services to sport

1995: wins Australian Three Day Event

2000: inducted into Sport Australia Hall of Fame

Gillian Rolton superstats

Olympic Results

1992 Barcelona Team	Gold
1996 Atlanta Team	Gold

Three-day event

Dressage: riders take their horses through thirty-six set movements to show how well they are able to control them.

Cross-country: riders take their horses over various surfaces, including roads, tracks, hills, obstacles and broken ground.

Jumping: riders take their horses over walls, rails and water jumps in as fast a time as possible.

☞ Guess what?

Gillian's horse, Peppermint Grove, is one of only two horses in the world to win back-to-back gold medals in the Three Day event.

Lionel Rose

One of Australia's best boxers and the first Aboriginal boxer to win a world championship

Full name: Lionel Edmund Rose

Born: 21 June 1948 in Jackson's Track, Victoria

Personal motto: Form comes and goes, but talent never leaves you.

Early years

Lionel grew up on an Aboriginal settlement at Jackson's Track, near Drouin, Victoria. The eldest of eight kids, he lived in a hut made out of old bits of roofing iron and timber offcuts from the nearby sawmill. Lionel loved hearing the stories his dad told him about the boxers he'd fought over the years in the tents of travelling sideshows. He and his mates collected some old fencing wire from the tip and set up their own boxing ring in the bush. They tied rags around their hands and danced around the ring, sparring like professional boxers.

☞ **Guess what?**

In 1996, Lionel gave the world title belt he won in 1968 to six-year-old Tjandamurra O'Shane. He hoped to inspire him to get over his injuries caused when he was doused with petrol and set alight in his schoolyard.

First fight

When Lionel was ten, he was taken on a trip to Melbourne by a charity that cared for underprivileged kids. He went to see his hero, Aboriginal boxer

George Bracken, fight at Festival Hall. Determined to become a champion boxer himself, the next year he began training at a local gym. He talked his trainer, Frank Oakes, into letting him fight in a junior boxing tournament in Sale before he was ready. Although he put up a brave fight, he was much smaller than his opponent, and was easily beaten.

On the road to success

Lionel kept battling away and by the time he was fifteen he'd become the national amateur flyweight champion. He moved to Melbourne and began living with his new trainer, Jack Rennie. Lionel had amazing balance and speed, a flashing left hook and brilliant reflexes. After missing out on being selected for the Aussie team for the 1964 Olympics, he turned professional. Two years later he won the Australian bantamweight title.

World champion

When Lionel was nineteen, he travelled to Japan to take on fighting legend Masahiko 'Fighting' Harada. The fight lasted for fifteen rounds. Despite an injured hand, Lionel outpointed the former champion to take home the World Bantamweight Title. He became the first Aboriginal sports star to win a world championship, and was declared a national hero. Nearly a

197

quarter of a million people lined the streets of Melbourne to welcome him home.

Role model

Lionel successfully defended his title three times before losing it in the fifth round of the 1969 title fight to Mexican knockout champion, 'Rockabye' Ruben Olivares. After an unsuccessful comeback attempt he retired from boxing in 1976. Finding it hard to cope with life outside the ring, he began drinking heavily and spent time in jail for various small crimes. Lionel soon managed to turn his life around, however. He took up a position with the Department of Aboriginal Affairs, coaching young sports stars and acting as a positive role model for Aboriginal people around the country.

Six interesting things about Lionel Rose

1 Lionel fought in fifty-three fights, and won forty-two of them.
2 His fight against Rocky Gattelari in 1967 was the first Australian boxing bout to be televised live interstate. When he won the fight he became a TV sports star.

3 In 1991, a mini-series about his life, 'Rose Against the Odds', was first broadcast on Australian television.

4 Elvis Presley was a big fan of his and once disguised himself so he could sit ringside to watch Lionel fight without being recognised.

5 He was famous for his huge smile.

6 In the 1970s, he released two hit songs: 'Thank You' and 'Pick Me up on Your Way Down'.

Career highlights

1963: becomes Australian amateur flyweight champion

1966: becomes Australian bantamweight champion

1968: wins the World Title against 'Fighting' Harada of Japan; becomes Australian of the Year; awarded an MBE for his services to sport.

Louise Sauvage

The best female wheelchair road-and-track racer in the world

Also known as: Lewis, Queen of the Track

Born: 18 September 1973 in Perth, Western Australia

Personal motto: You never know what you can do or achieve until you try.

Website: www.aspire.au.com

Early years

Louise was born in 1973 with a severe spinal disability. By the time she was ten, she'd had twenty-one operations. She started swimming when she was three to build up her upper body strength, which she would need to use a wheelchair. Louise loved swimming, and dreamt of becoming a champion. However, when she was fourteen she had steel rods inserted into her back to help fix a curve in her spine. She was told to keep away from sport for two years, and when she finally returned she found the rods interfered with her ability to swim. Never one to give up, Louise switched to wheelchair racing instead.

A new sport

Louise had been involved in wheelchair sports since she was eight. Now her dream of becoming a champion Paralympic swimmer was over, she put all her effort and concentration into her new sport. In 1990, when she was sixteen, she represented Australia at the Disabled Athletics World Championships in Holland. She won the 100-metre event, setting a new world record. Two years later she completed her first major road race, then won four medals at the Paralympic Games in Barcelona, earning herself the title 'Queen of the Track'.

Champion racer

After her success at Barcelona, Louise began training for long-distance events. Between 1994 and 2001 she won ten marathons, including her heart-stopping feat in the 1998 Boston Marathon. Louise overtook seven-time winner Jean Driscoll from 50 metres behind to win the race in a photo finish. She picked up more gold medals at the Atlanta and Sydney Paralympic and Olympic Games, making her the undisputed champion of wheelchair racing in the world. During her career she has played a huge role in helping to change people's views about people with disabilities.

Louise Sauvage superstats

1992 Barcelona Paralympic Games
Gold: 100 m, 200 m, 400 m; Silver: 800 m
1996 Atlanta Paralympic Games
Gold: 400 m, 800 m, 1500 m, 5000 m
1996 Atlanta Olympic Games
Gold: 800 m demonstration event
2000 Sydney Paralympic Games
Gold: 500 m, 1500 m; Silver: 800 m
2000 Sydney Olympic Games
Gold: 800 m demonstration event

World Records

200 m, 1500 m, 5000 m, 4 × 100 m relay, 4 × 400 m relay

Marathons

10 (between 1994 and 1999)

Career highlights

1992:   receives Order of Australia Medal

1993:   ABC Sports Star of the Year

1994:   Australian Paralympian of the Year (also 1996, 1997 and 1998)

1997:   Australian Institute of Sport Athlete of the Year

1998:   Young Australian of the Year

1999:   Australian Female Athlete of the Year

2000:   wins Sydney Host City Marathon

☞ Guess what?

During the 800-metres final at the Sydney 2000 Paralympics, half the competitors crashed into each other. The Canadian team successfully appealed against the decision to rerun the race, and Louise came second to her arch-rival, Chantal Petitclerc.

Catherine Helen Spence

A writer and a champion of women's and children's rights

Also known as: The Grand Old Woman of Australia

Born: 31 October 1825, Melrose, Scotland

Died: 3 April 1910, South Australia

Banknote: $5

Early years

Catherine was born in Scotland, the fifth of eight children. When she was thirteen her father lost all his money through bad investments. Thinking he could make a better life in the new colonies, he borrowed some more funds and took his family to Australia on the *Palmyra*, settling in South Australia. During the long journey, Catherine, who'd been educated at an Academy for Young Ladies, gave lessons to other kids on the ship.

Teacher, author and journalist

Life in the new colony was hard. When she was seventeen, Catherine found work as a governess to help support her family. Three years later, with the assistance of her mother and sister, and glowing references from her teachers in Scotland, she opened her own school. In 1848 Catherine began a long career as a journalist and critic. Many of her articles were about political and social issues of the time, such as equal opportunity for women. She also began to write novels. The first, *Clara Morison: A Tale of South Australia during the Gold Fever*, was published in 1854. Over the next thirty years she wrote six more, including *Tender and True* (1856), *Mr Hogarth's Will* (1865) and *Gathered In* (1881).

Looking out for the poor

In the 1860s, Catherine began to take an interest in the treatment of underprivileged children. In those days, orphans and abandoned children were kept in institutions, in shocking conditions. In 1872, Catherine and a group of friends set up the Boarding Out Society, which helped to place children into homes that offered them a stable family life. Realising that education was important for women to escape the poverty trap, she also helped set up kindergartens and secondary schools for girls. Once they had a basic education, women could finally go on to teachers' training colleges and university, something that had not been possible before.

👉 Guess what?

Catherine's book about women and marriage, **Handfasted**, wasn't published until 1984 – over seventy years after she died. She wanted the laws that kept married women financially dependent on their husbands changed. Publishers back then thought that if people read the book, it might cause marriage breakdowns.

Votes for women

Catherine worked for fifty years to change Australia's voting system. She aimed to bring in a system of proportional voting, which she called 'effective voting'. She travelled around Australia, Britain and America, giving lectures on her ideas. In 1894, helped along by her hard work, South Australia became the first State in Australia to give women the vote. Three years later, Catherine became the first woman to stand for an elected political seat. Although she didn't make the cut, she continued to campaign for voting changes. Catherine, who never married, spent the last years of her life writing her autobiography. She died in 1910, aged eighty-five.

Four interesting things about Catherine Helen Spence

1 She had to use her brother's name, or simply her initials, when she wrote her articles because it wasn't considered acceptable for women to write for newspapers in those days. She also published her first two books anonymously.

2 She was the first woman in Australia to become a professional journalist, and wrote

for various newspapers for more than
sixty years.

3 She brought up three families of orphaned
children by herself.

4 She wrote the first ever high school social
studies text book, *The Laws We Live Under*.

Career highlights

1846: opens her own school

1854: her first book is published

1861: begins her political career by writing a
pamphlet about effective voting

1872: sets up the Boarding Out Society to help
find homes for poor women and children

1893: travels to USA and Canada to give lectures
on effective voting

1894: women in South Australia gain the vote

1897: becomes Australia's first woman political
candidate

Andy Thomas

The first Australian to go into space

Full name: Andrew Sydney Withiel Thomas

Born: 18 December 1951 in Adelaide,
South Australia

Website:
http://home.vicnet.net.au/~gormandale/oz-astro.htm

Early years

When Andy was six, he and his dad used to search the evening sky for the bright light of *Sputnik I* as it whizzed past on its orbit around the Earth. Russia's *Sputnik I* was Earth's first artificial satellite. After that, Andy was determined to become a spaceman, like the characters in his comic books. He spent hours in his bedroom, painting and gluing together plastic model spacecraft.

Watching the moonwalk

Andy kept up his interest in space throughout his time at school, following the race between the United States and the Russians to see who would be the first to send people into space. He stayed home from uni the day Neil Armstrong became the first person to walk on the moon so he could watch the moon-landing live on TV. Andy graduated from the University of Adelaide in 1972, with first-class honours in mechanical engineering. He continued his studies in Adelaide, winning a prize for his research into aerodynamics.

First trip

Andy took up a job offer with the Lockheed Corporation in Georgia, in the United States, eventually becoming manager of its Flight Services Division. In

October 1992, he was accepted into the space shuttle program at NASA. He and eighteen other candidates had been chosen out of 2,054 applicants. Andy spent a year in Houston finding out everything there was to know about the space shuttle and how it worked. On 19 May 1996, Andy boarded the *Endeavour* for a nine-day mission as Payload Commander, in charge of scientific experiments.

Life on Mir

In 1998, Andy climbed aboard the *Endeavour* once again, and took off for Mir, the Russian space station, which was hosting NASA astronauts. During his 141 days in space, Andy travelled over 90 million kilometres. He made 2,250 orbits of the Earth, experiencing 16 sunrises each day. Because he was living at zero gravity, everyday actions like eating and washing his hair became much trickier to do. 'Loose' water explodes into droplets and floats around the cabin, so he had to use no-rinse shampoo that could be towelled out of his hair, drink from a straw inserted into a sealed bag, and keep his lips tight around his toothbrush while brushing his teeth.

Coming down to Earth

After nearly five months in space, it took Andy a long time to get used to living with gravity again. He felt like he was walking around with bags of weights on his arms and legs, and had to spend hours with a physiotherapist, getting rid of the aches and pains in his muscles. In March 2001, Andy headed back into space on the *Discovery* for a twelve-day mission to the International Space Station. He is currently Deputy Chief of the Astronaut Office at NASA.

Andy's daily schedule on Space Station Mir

- Get up (8.30 a.m.), wash face, shave, brush teeth
- Breakfast (scrambled eggs, bread, juice and coffee)
- Receive radiogram that outlines work tasks for the day
- Conduct scientific experiments
- Break for exercise on treadmill and stretching arm and leg muscles (1.00 p.m.)
- Float over to a window and listen quietly to music while watching the Earth pass by
- Lunch with crewmates
- More experiments, or 'housework'
- Dinner and a video with crewmates (7.00 p.m.)

- Write letters, answer kids' emails, read, watch Earth pass the window
- Go to bed in floating sleeping bags tied to a wall or the floor (11.00 p.m.)

Andy's tips on how to become an astronaut

Get a good education and enjoy the work that you do. NASA is interested in people who have studied technical subjects such as engineering, science, physics or medicine at an advanced level.

Andy's spaceflights

Mission	Craft	Dates	Duration
STS-77	Endeavour	19.05. – 29.05.1996	10 days 00 hours 40 minutes
STS-89	Mir	23.01. – 12.06.1998	140 days 15 hours 13 minutes
STS-102	International Space Station	08.03. – 21.03.2001	12 days 19 hours 49 minutes

Ian Thorpe

One of the world's most successful swimmers

Full name: Ian James Thorpe

Also known as: Thorpedo, Thorpey

Born: 13 October 1982 in Sydney,
New South Wales

Website: www.ianthorpe.telstra.com.au

Early years

Ian grew up in south-western Sydney. He loved playing ball games and running around in the bush with his friends, pretending to be Tarzan. He also enjoyed building cubby houses and constructing complicated designs with Lego. He had some swimming lessons when he was young, but it was his sister Christina who was the swimmer in the family – Ian was allergic to chlorine! He played soccer and went to Little Athletics instead.

Joining the squad

Ian spent so much time sitting by the side of the pool watching Christina and his friends swim in swimming carnivals, he figured he might as well start swimming competitively too. He joined the squad at Padstow Pool when he was eight, and by the end of the year had won his first medal. Ian kept up his soccer and athletics for a couple of years, but all that training soon became too much for him. He decided to concentrate on swimming, wearing a nose plug to help his chlorine allergy.

A new world champion

By the time he was fourteen, Ian had joined the national team, winning a silver medal at the 1997 Pan Pacific Championships for the 400-metres freestyle. The next year he became the youngest ever male

Olympics • swimming • design • tv

world champion in swimming when he won the same event at the World Championships in Perth. Over the following years, Ian stunned the world with his ability to win races, bringing home fistfuls of gold medals and world record titles.

> ☞ Guess what?
>
> In the moments before a race, rather than trying to psych himself up, Ian tries to relax by thinking of anything but swimming.

Life outside the pool

Ian takes time out of his busy schedule to promote fundraising projects for leukaemia and cancer research, and set up his own foundation to help support sick kids. He donated the $25,000 prize money he won for breaking the first ever record at the new Sydney Aquatic Centre to charity. In recent years, he has begun a TV career, appearing on shows such as 'Undercover Angels'. He is also interested in fashion and jewellery design.

Ian's training schedule

Five mornings a week, Ian's alarm pulls him out of bed at 4.17 a.m., and he is in the pool by 5.00 a.m. for a two-and-a-half-hour session. He also trains five afternoons each week, and squeezes weight training, boxing and yoga into his schedule. Wednesday mornings he gets to sleep in, and he hangs out with friends and family on Saturday afternoons and Sundays. When he's preparing for a swimming season, Ian spends three weeks 'over-training' to build up his endurance, churning up 100 kilometres a week in the pool.

Ian Thorpe superstats

1   He broke 22 world records before he turned twenty.
2   He was the youngest male swimmer ever to swim for Australia.
3   He currently holds the world record for the 200-, 400- and 800-metres freestyle, and is a member of the world record relay team for both the 4 × 100 and 4 × 200 metres freestyle.
4   He has won 3 gold and 2 silver Olympic medals, 10 gold Commonwealth Games medals and 8 World Championship titles.
5   At the 2001 World Championships at Fukuoka, Japan, he won 6 gold medals – 4 of them in world-record time – something

that no other swimmer has ever achieved before.

6 He is 192 centimetres tall, weighs ninety-seven kilograms, has 7 per cent body fat, and wears size seventeen shoes. Some swimming experts believe his large feet give him a competitive edge because they act like flippers.

Career highlights

1998: awarded USA Swimming Magazine World Swimmer of the Year

1999: awarded Australian Swimmer of the Year and Male Athlete of the Year; wins the Don Bradman Award for the 'Athlete who has most inspired the nation'

2000: awarded Young Australian of the Year

2001: becomes Telstra Australian Swimmer of the Year for the third year in a row

2002: becomes the first Australian to win the American International Athlete Trophy for the World's Most Outstanding Athlete

Truganini

A Tasmanian Aborigine of the Palawah people

Also known as: Princess Lalla Rookh, Trucanini, Trugernanner

Born: around 1812 in Recherche Bay, Van Diemen's Land

Died: 8 May 1876 in Hobart, Tasmania

Early years

Truganini was born in the Bruny Island-D'Entrecasteaux Channel area of Van Diemen's Land (now known as Tasmania). Her father, Mangana, was a local chief. His people had lived a simple life for thousands of years, moving around from place to place in search of food. This had all changed in 1803, when European settlers came to the area. They cut down trees, built houses and planted crops. Fights broke out between the local people and the newcomers, and over the following years hundreds of Aboriginal people were killed.

Rape and murder

By the time she was seventeen Truganini's mother and uncle had been murdered by whalers. Truganini was raped, and her sisters taken away as slaves by men who had come to hunt seals on the island. When Truganini's husband-to-be, Paraweena, tried to rescue her from a convict camp, he was brutally attacked with a hatchet and left to drown in the channel.

The Friendly Mission

By 1830, the fighting between the two groups had become so widespread that it became known as the 'Black War'. Only 300 of the original 4,000 Aboriginal people were left. The authorities decided that something had to be done to stop the killing. They sent George Robinson, a builder and preacher, to the area on what was called a 'Friendly Mission'. His job was to find the remaining Aboriginal people who were hiding deep in the bush, and move them to Flinders Island, where they could live in safety.

☞ Guess what?

Although for many years Truganini was spoken of as 'the last Tasmanian Aborigine', this isn't true. Today there are several thousand people still living in Tasmania who are descendants of the early tribes living there.

A guiding hand

George persuaded Truganini and her father to come with him by promising them that their customs would be respected, and that they would be still able to visit their homeland. Realising that George's offer was the only way her people could survive the constant massacres, Truganini and her husband Wooraddy agreed to help him find the remaining Aboriginal people. Over the next five years she and her friends guided George through the bush and showed him how to find food. They also protected him from attacks from the people hiding in the bush.

A bad mistake

By 1835, nearly all the Aboriginal people had agreed to move to a settlement at Wybelanna on Flinders Island. Although George hoped to be able to teach them European ways and improve their standard of living, many saw their new home as a prison, and became sick and died. Truganini now realised she had made a mistake helping the white man, and stopped encouraging people to move to the new settlement. She also refused to help George when he took her and a group of others to Melbourne, hoping they would help to 'civilise' the 'savage' Aboriginal people from the Port Phillip area.

Returning home

Truganini was sent back to Wybelanna, but by now it was obvious the settlement had failed. In 1847, she and the remaining forty-five people were moved to Oyster Cove on the Tasmanian mainland. Although conditions here were even worse than those on Flinders Island, Truganini was happier. The land here was her traditional territory, and she was able to go hunting and visit places that were special to her.

Truganini spent her last years in Hobart, and died in 1876, aged sixty-four. Although she asked to be buried in the mountains, her skeleton was hung on display in the Tasmanian Museum in Hobart for 100 years. In 1976, her bones were cremated and her ashes spread over the waters of her birth place.

Three interesting things about Truganini

1 She saved George Robinson's life during an attack by floating him across a river on a log.

2 While she was living on Flinders Island she refused to live by 'white man's ways', preferring to hold on to the traditional way of life that her father had taught her.

3 When she was living in Hobart she became a well-known person around town. She liked to wear a bright red cap. It reminded her of the colour her people had traditionally worn their hair, using dyes made from red gum leaves or ochre.

Nancy Wake

A hero who helped the French resistance fighters during World War II

Full name: Nancy Grace Augusta Wake

Also known as: The White Mouse

Born: 30 August 1912 in Wellington, New Zealand

Early years

Nancy was the youngest of six children. When she was two, her father took a job as editor on an Australian newspaper, and the Wakes moved to Sydney. Nancy was always her dad's favourite child, and she spent many happy hours sitting on his lap listening to music or reading stories with him. When her father walked out on the family one day, they were forced to move to a smaller house in a less fancy suburb.

The dream

Nancy dreamed of living somewhere much more glamorous – a city like London, Paris or New York. She started saving for her trip when she was eight, selling off the chokos from her garden to the greengrocer to raise funds. By the age of sixteen, she was so fed up with fighting with her mum she climbed out of the window of the house she hated so much and ran away to the country to become a nurse. In 1932, when she was twenty, her aunt unexpectedly sent her some money, and she sailed to London – via New York – to finally live her dream.

War breaks out

A year later, Nancy tricked her way into a job as a journalist in Paris. She visited Austria and Germany when Hitler came to power, and saw firsthand how cruelly the

Nazis were treating Jewish people. In 1939, Nancy married a French millionaire named Henri Fiocca. Six months later, Germany invaded France. Many people fled their homes to escape the soldiers, but were killed by German planes. When Nancy saw what was happening, she was determined to help in any way she could.

> ☞ Guess what?
>
> Nancy is currently living rent-free in a posh hotel in Piccadilly, London. Although her bill each year is more than $200,000, she has no money to pay it. When Prince Charles read her biography, he was so inspired by her life he offered to help out with the bill.

The White Mouse

Nancy began working as a courier for the French Resistance, a secret network of groups of people who fought behind the scenes to overthrow the Germans occupying France. Her group helped Jewish families and British pilots who'd been shot down over France to escape. Nancy soon became the number one target of the Gestapo, who called her 'the White Mouse' because whenever she was cornered, she'd manage to slip away. Knowing she'd be killed if they caught her, Nancy escaped over the mountains to Spain, eventually making it back to London. Her husband was tortured and killed when he refused to tell the Gestapo where she was.

Nancy the spy

Nancy spent the next year training to become a spy. She was parachuted back into France in 1944, along with other members of the Special Operations Executive. Working with a radio operator, her job was to make contact with the various groups of Resistance fighters hiding in the forests, and to arrange for supplies of weapons to be dropped to them. By 1944, the sabotage efforts of the Resistance movement were starting to pay off, and the German army was forced out of France. A year later, the war ended. Nancy received many medals for her bravery. After living in Australia for years with little recognition, she returned to London in 2001, where she is adored by her many fans.

Four interesting things about Nancy Wake

1 When she was seven, her brother dared her to jump off the roof – so she did. She told

him that she never stopped to think about what might happen if she took up a dare, because that would scare her off and stop her from trying it.

2 Her favourite books were *Anne of Green Gables* and *Anne of the Island* by Lucy Maud Montgomery. She loved the character of Anne Shirley and wanted to be just like her, having loads of adventures and living an interesting life away from her family.

3 While working for the French Resistance, the radio they used to contact London each night was lost during an attack by the Germans. Nancy dressed up as a local girl and rode a bicycle for 200 kilometres to different villages until she found an operator who could help them.

4 Aussie actor Cate Blanchett starred in a film inspired by her life, *Charlotte Gray*, in 2002.

Shane Warne

One of the greatest and most controversial players in the history of cricket

Full name: Shane Keith Warne

Also known as: Warney, Hollywood

Born: 13 September 1969 in Melbourne, Victoria

Early years

Shane grew up playing cricket in the driveway of his home in Black Rock with his younger brother Jason. Hitting the wall at the back of the house meant they were out, and the fence became the wicket-keeper. The brothers had to get each other out ten times, and keep track of their runs and wickets on a scorecard. They pretended to be famous players, and each time they bowled, they imitated a particular bowler's style.

First games

Shane was soon playing Saturday morning cricket with the East Sandringham Under-12 and Under-14 sides. Although he started out as a fast bowler, he was fascinated by the amazing things spin bowlers could do with a ball, and asked one of the players from the First XI to give him some tips on bowling leg-breaks. He was also a big hitter and it soon became obvious he was going to be useful as an all-rounder.

Footy vs cricket

Shane was also a talented footballer. When he was eighteen he joined the St Kilda football club, playing a season with the Under-19s. The next summer he played cricket for the St Kilda Second XI. It was time to make a choice between the two games, and he chose cricket, heading off to England to play for a club in Gloucestershire. He returned with loads of experience and was soon selected for the St Kilda First XI. After a successful tour of the West Indies with the Australian youth team, Shane was invited to join the Australian Cricket Academy in Adelaide.

Cricketer of the Year

In 1991, Shane played his first game for Victoria. The next year he made his Test debut for Australia. By the time the 1994–95 season came around he was firing, taking 8 wickets for 71 runs in the second innings of the First Test. In the next match, he bowled the first hat trick (three wickets in a row) in an Ashes series for ninety years, earning himself the title of 1994 Wisden Cricketer of the Year. In 2000, he was named in cricketing almanac Wisden as one of the top five cricketers of the century after he broke Dennis Lillee's record for the number of wickets taken in Test matches.

A colourful career

Shane has always been one of the most colourful players in the game, famous for his bleached blond hair, zinc-creamed nose and lips, diamond stud earring and wraparound sunnies. He frequently hits the headlines, for issues ranging from playing up while on tour to battles with his weight. In 1998, he got into trouble for accepting money from an Indian bookmaker in return for information on weather conditions at Australian grounds. In early 2003, Shane bounced back from a serious shoulder injury in time for the new Test season. However, after a positive test for a banned drug, he received a one-year suspension from the game.

Six amazing things about Shane Warne

1 He is the fifth highest wicket-taker in One-Day International history.

2 He is Test cricket's second highest wicket-taker, with 491 victims.

3 In 1998, he broke the record for the most number of wickets taken in Test matches by a spin bowler.

4 During 1999–2000 season, he broke Dennis Lillee's record of 355 Test wickets taken.

5 He is famous for his top spinner, his googly, and his favourite ball – the flipper.

6 He has inspired kids all over Australia to change from fast to spin bowling.

Career highlights

1990:   enters Australian Cricket Academy

1991:   makes first-class debut for Victoria against Western Australia

1992:   makes Test debut for Australia against India

1993:   first ball bowled in game against England makes cricketing history

1994:   becomes Wisden Cricketer of the Year

1999:   selected as Man of the Match in Australia's World Cup final victory

2000:   selected as one of five Wisden cricketers of the century

The ball from hell

In 1993, during his first match against England, Shane bowled the most famous ball in the history of cricket. His first delivery of the match was to Mike Gatting, the former English captain. The ball floated down the pitch like a silent bomb, dipping sharply to the right at the last moment to knock out the wicket. Gatting was so stunned he had to ask the umpire to confirm that he was out.

Karrie Webb

One of the best female golfers in the world

Full name: Karrie Anne Webb

Also known as: Hookie, Tigress

Born: 21 December 1974 in Ayr, Queensland

Early years

Both Karrie's grandparents played golf, and four-year-old Karrie used to trail around behind them on the local golf course, hitting a plastic ball with a plastic club. When she was eight, they gave her a cut-down set of golf clubs, and she was soon hooked, spending all her spare time out on the course. Two years later she told her grandfather that she was going to be the best golfer in the world.

Meeting her idol

It was after a trip to Brisbane to see her idol, Greg Norman, play in the Queensland Open that Karrie knew what she wanted to do: become a professional golfer. She began to enter amateur competitions and by the time she was sixteen she'd won both the North Queensland Open and the Australian Schoolgirls Championship. A win in a junior tournament saw her jetting off to the States to spend a week with Greg and his family in Florida. Greg was so impressed with her skill and determination to work hard that he predicted a great future for her.

Turning pro

Three years later, Karrie turned professional, and left Australia to try her luck overseas. Her brilliant form soon saw her ranked in the world's top ten, and earned her the title 'Rookie of the Year'. The next year, she surprised everyone by winning the British Open. She then went to the USA to qualify for a ranking in the LPGA (Ladies' Professional Golf Association). Karrie finished second out of the 160 qualifiers.

☞ Guess what?

In 2001, although her grandfather had just suffered a massive stroke, Karrie decided to play in a major US tournament rather than return home to visit him, because she knew he would have wanted her to play. She won the tournament, and in doing so became the youngest player ever to win a career Grand Slam.

The road to success

Over the next few years, Karrie continued to dominate the international tournament circuit. By 1999, she was ranked number one in the world, and had taken home several trophies for having the lowest season scoring average. She also became the first woman to win over 1 million US dollars in prize money in one season. After cleaning up most of the world's major women's events in 2000, sports analysts put her on a par with men's champion Tiger Woods. Karrie and Tiger are now considered to be the greatest female and male golfers in the history of the game.

Six interesting things about Karrie Webb

1 When she was twelve months old she pulled a metal-rimmed pot plant off a table and broke her nose. After that, her family called her 'Hookie'.

2 When her lifelong coach, Kelvin Haller, was injured in an accident and confined to a wheelchair, Karrie refused to let him go. She keeps up her lessons via the Internet, emailing him videos of her swing. He studies them, then gives her advice over the phone.

3 She is often criticised for not smiling while on the course.

4 She created her own clothing company in 1996.

5 She is superstitious and uses different numbered balls on different days: Thursday, number four, Friday three, Saturday two, and Sunday one.

6 An official at the 1995 British Open used a mobile phone to keep her family and friends back home up to date on her score.

Career highlights

1990: wins Australian Schoolgirls Championship

1994: turns professional

1995: wins British Open and becomes European Tour Rookie of the Year

1996: Rolex Rookie of the Year

1997: wins first LPGA Vare Trophy for lowest season scoring average

1999: wins Rolex Player of the Year; ranked Number One in the world

2000: wins her first Australian Open; scores the hat-trick for three consecutive Australian Masters titles; wins Female Athlete of the Year

2002: becomes first player to win five different major titles

Judith Wright

One of Australia's leading poets, and also a conservationist and an activist for Aboriginal rights

Full name: Judith Arundell Wright

Born: 31 May 1915 near Armidale, New South Wales

Died: 25 June 2000 in Canberra, ACT

Early years

A fifth generation Australian, Judith was born at Wallamumbi, a property in northern New South Wales. She loved being outdoors, following the stockmen around the property and riding horses. She always felt very close to the land where she lived, and years later wrote about the trees and the birds, the rocks and the creeks that she saw every day when she was young. When Judith was twelve, her mother died of influenza, and she was sent to boarding school in Armidale.

☞ Guess what?

On her eightieth birthday Judith recorded an interview for the TV show, 'The 7.30 Report'. However, it was so critical of the government's treatment of the environment and Aboriginal people, it never went to air.

Study and work

After finishing school, Judith went on to study Arts at Sydney University, determined to be a writer. She studied Aboriginal culture and society, and wrote articles and poems for the student newspaper and magazines. After nine months of travel overseas, she returned to Sydney to work as a secretary for a professor at the University. When World War II broke out, Judith worked for a time at the Sydney Air Raid Precautions Centre, before returning to Wallamumbi to help her father run the property while her brothers were fighting overseas.

First books

Back home again, Judith began to write poetry about the land she loved so strongly. Her first collection of poetry, *The Moving Image*, was published in 1946 to great acclaim. People thought of her as a major new talent. She was given a Commonwealth Fund Literary scholarship which helped her to write *The Generations of Men*, a book about her grandfather, and his life as a pioneer farmer in outback Queensland.

Respect for another culture

Over the years, Judith wrote many more collections of poetry. She also wrote several kids' books, such as *Kings of the Dingoes*, the story of three farm dogs who gang together to defeat the leader of a dingo pack. She felt a great bond with Aboriginal people, and had a deep respect for their culture. She was good friends with Oodgeroo Noonuccal, and helped her to

writing • conservation • activism

become the first Aboriginal poet to be published in English. Several of Judith's books gave her views on the unjust treatment she believed Aboriginal people have received from white settlers.

For the love of her land

In the early 1960s, Judith fought to save the Great Barrier Reef, and with a group of friends, she set up the Wildlife Preservation Society in Brisbane. She also started a conservation magazine, *Wildlife in Australia*. Over the years, Judith has received many distinguished awards for her writing, including the honour of becoming the first Australian to receive the Queen's Gold Medal for Poetry. She continued to support environmental concerns and Aboriginal rights throughout her life, taking part in a march for reconciliation a month before her death in 2000.

Three interesting things about Judith Wright

1 When she was little, she used to take her younger brothers to a group of rocks on a hill near her house, because she thought the rocks had special powers. She used to strike the rocks with a piece of iron until a spark

came out, which was a sign that she had magical powers and her brothers must therefore obey her.

2 Her favourite book when she was growing up was *My Brilliant Career*, by Miles Franklin. She thought she was like Sybylla, the main character in the book, because they both saw writing as a way to escape into a world outside their own experience.

3 When she was seventeen, the new pony she was riding had a heart attack and crashed to the ground on top of her. She spent three months in hospital with a broken pelvis.

Seven books by Judith Wright

The Moving Image (1946)

Kings of the Dingoes (1959)

The Generations of Men (1959)

The Day the Mountains Played (1963)

The Cry for the Dead (1981)

The Coral Battlefield (1977)

Half a Lifetime (1999)

Nat Young

One of the world's greatest surfers

Full name: Robert Harold Young

Also known as: Gnat, Animal

Born: 14 November 1947 in Sydney,
New South Wales

Website: www.natyoung.com

Early years

Nat Young grew up in the coastal suburb of Collaroy, between two famous surf breaks – North Narrabeen and Dee Why. His backyard was the beach. He rode his first real wave on an inflatable Surfoplane – an ancestor of the boogie board. After school and on weekends he used to collect the soft drink bottles left behind on the beach and cash them in for the deposit money. He also enjoyed collecting 'treasures' from the rockpools along the beach.

His first board

When he was nine, Nat and his best friend Henry started hanging around the surf club, fetching drinks and snacks from the shop for their heroes – the bronzed guys on surf patrol. The lifesavers used to call the younger boys 'gremlins' or 'gremmies'. Nat spent hours watching the older boys surf, and was rapt when his mum bought him a second-hand Malibu board for his tenth birthday. He was soon spending every minute he could out in the surf.

From gremmie to champion

By the time he was sixteen Nat had graduated from being the smallest gremmie on the beach to the winner of the 1963 Australian Open Men's title. He was now two metres tall, with long, powerful arms and legs that enabled him to move like a shark through the biggest of waves. Rival Midget Farrelly won the World Championships at Manly Beach the next year. His win kicked off a lifelong feud between the two surfers, spurring Nat on to take out the next world contest in 1966 on his new board, 'Sam'.

☞ Guess what?

Nat was brutally assaulted in 2000 while surfing at his local beach. It inspired him to put together the book **Surf Rage** – a collection of articles about the violence that erupts on overcrowded surf beaches.

The animal

In the late 1960s and early 1970s, Nat began riding shortboards. His ruthless, aggressive style soon earned him a new nickname – Animal. He continued to win contests, riding five-metre waves to take out the unofficial world championships on Hawaii's north shore. He returned to longboards in the 80s, picking up another four world championship titles. Surfing has been Nat's world for over forty years. He has run a surf shop and design business and has written five books, including *The History of Surfing*, which was made into a movie in 1985. He currently lives – and surfs – at Angourie, on the northern coast of New South Wales, with his wife and kids.

Four interesting things about Nat Young

1 He was so small as a kid, he used to have to get his dad to carry his surfboard over the sand to the water for him. Later, he built a trolley for it out of bits of wood and the wheels off an old pram.

2 The name he's used for most of his life comes from the nickname the other surfers gave him when he first started surfing: 'Gnat'. His huge board was called the 'Queen Mary' after the biggest ship in the world at that time. The other surfers all reckoned he was so small, he looked like a gnat on the end of the *Queen Mary*. 'Gnat' eventually became 'Nat'.

3 He has won four Australian Longboard Championships titles and five World titles. In 2000 his son Beau proved he was a 'chip

off the old block' by becoming World Champion himself.

4 Inspired by Midnight Oil singer and environmentalist Peter Garrett, and keen to clean up Sydney's polluted beaches, he stood for a seat in State Parliament in the 1980s, narrowly missing out on being elected.

Five books by Nat Young

Nat Young's Book Of Surfing (1979)
Surfing Australia's East Coast (1980)
The History of Surfing (1983)
Surfing Fundamentals (1985)
Nat's Nat and That's That (1998)

Career highlights

1963:   wins his first Australian Open Men's title

1964:   wins the junior division of the World Longboard Championships at Manly Beach, Sydney

1966:   wins his first World Longboard Championships in San Diego, California

1990:   becomes World Longboard Champion for the fifth time

Want more?

Try your local bookshop or library for these books about your favourite famous Australians.

ROBYN ARCHER
Costain, M. *Robyn Archer: performer, writer, director*, Heinemann Library, 1997
RON BARASSI
Barassi, R. & McFarline, P. *Barassi: the life behind the legend*, Simon & Schuster, 1995
DON BRADMAN
Chase, D. & Krantz, K. *Don Bradman: a cricketing legend*, Macmillan, 1991
ROBERT O'HARA BURKE
Murgatroyd, S. *The Dig Tree: the story of Burke and Wills*, Text Publishing, 2002
Clune, F. *Dig!: the Burke and Wills saga*, Angus & Robertson, 1981
Flynn, R. *Burke and Wills: crossing the continent*, Macmillan, 1991
Jensen, J. *Burke and Wills*, Future Horizons Publishing, 1996
VICTOR CHANG
Chang, V. *Victor Chang: a tribute to my father*, Pan Macmillan, 2001

Hall, R. *Tiger General: the killing of Victor Chang*, Pan Macmillan, 1995

CAROLINE CHISHOLM

Flynn, R. *Caroline Chisholm: the emigrant's friend*, Macmillan, 1991

Steele, R. *Caroline Chisholm: the emigrant's friend*, Reed Library-Cardigan Street, 1996

EDWARD 'WEARY' DUNLOP

Higgins, D. *Weary Dunlop: doctor, diplomat and saviour*, CIS Cardigan Street, 1996

MATTHEW FLINDERS

Dodson, C. *Bass and Flinders*, Scholastic, 1999

Scott, E. *The Life of Matthew Flinders*, Angus & Robertson, 2001

HOWARD FLOREY

Murray, K. *Howard Florey: miracle maker*, Allen & Unwin, 1998

ERROL FLYNN

Bret, D. *Errol Flynn: Satan's Angel*, Robson Books, 2000

JOHN FLYNN

Rudolph, I. *John Flynn: of flying doctors and frontier faith*, Central Queensland University Press, 2000

DAWN FRASER

Sedunary, A. *Dawn Fraser: Australian swimming legend*, Reed Library-Cardigan Street, 1996

CATHY FREEMAN

Dolan, B. *Cathy Freeman*, Heinemann Library, 1997

Russell, J. *Cathy Freeman*, Heinemann Library, 2002

MAY GIBBS

Walsh, M. *May Gibbs: mother of the gumnuts*, Angus & Robertson, 1985

PERCY GRAINGER

Bird, J. *Percy Grainger*, Currency Press, 1998

GERMAINE GREER

Britain, I. *Once an Australian: journeys with Clive James, Barry Humphries, Germaine Greer and Robert Hughes*, OUP, 1997

FRED HOLLOWS

Butler, M. *Fred Hollows*, CIS Cardigan Street, 1995

BARRY HUMPHRIES

Humphries, B. *My Life As Me: a memoir*, Penguin, 2002

Lahr, J. *Dame Edna Everage and the rise of Western civilisation*, Bloomsbury, 1991

PAUL JENNINGS

Ricketson, M. *Paul Jennings: the boy in the story is always me*, Penguin, 2000

NED KELLY

Jones, I. *Ned Kelly: a short life*, Lothian, 1995

Kelly, Ned *The Jerilderie Letter*, Text, 2001

McMenomy, K. *Ned Kelly: the authentic illustrated history*, Hardie Grant Books, 2001

Wilkinson, C. *Black Snake: The daring of Ned Kelly*, black dog books, 2002

NICOLE KIDMAN

Ewbank, T. & Hildred, S. *Nicole Kidman: the biography*, Headline, 2002

CHARLES KINGSFORD SMITH

Hughes, W. *Charles Kingsford Smith*, Hodder & Stoughton, 1986

WALLY LEWIS

McGregor, A. *King Wally and the Broncos*, UQP, 1989

NORMAN LINDSAY

Bloomfield, L. (ed.) *The World of Norman Lindsay*, Macmillan, 1979

MARY MACKILLOP

Goodwin, J. *Mary MacKillop: a great Australian*, Dove Communications, 1985

Inserra, R. *Mary MacKillop: Holy Mother to the poor*, CIS Cardigan St, 1995

JESSE MARTIN

Martin, J. *Lionheart: the Jesse Martin story*, Allen & Unwin, 2000

DOUGLAS MAWSON

Krantz, V & Chase, D. *Douglas Mawson: Antarctic Explorer*, Macmillan, 1991

Magee, A. *Douglas Mawson*, Heinemann Library, 1996

NELLIE MELBA

Magee, A. Nellie *Melba: the Australian diva*, CIS Cardigan St, 1995

Irvine, N. *Nellie Melba*, Hodder & Stoughton, 1986

KYLIE MINOGUE

Stanley-Clarke, J & Goodall, N. *Kylie Naked*, Ebury Press, 2002

HARRY 'BREAKER' MORANT

Bleszynski, N. *Shoot Straight, You Bastards!: the truth behind the killing of Breaker Morant*, Random House, 2002

Cutlack, F.M. *Breaker Morant: a horseman who made history*, Ure Smith, 1962

JOHNNY O'KEEFE

Bryden-Brown, J. *J O'K: the official Johnny O'Keefe story*, Doubleday, 1992

Johnstone, D. *The Wild One: the life and times of Johnny O'Keefe*, Allen & Unwin, 2001

BANJO PATERSON
Blake, W. *Banjo Paterson: poet of the bush*, Macmillan, 1991

GILLIAN ROLTON
Rolton, G. *Free Rein: the autobiography of an Olympic heroine*, HarperCollins, 2003

LOUISE SAUVAGE
Sheppard, B. *Louise Sauvage*, Heinemann Library, 2002

ANDY THOMAS
Burgess, C. *Australia's Astronauts: three men and a spaceflight dream*, Kangaroo Press, 1999

IAN THORPE
Thorpe, I. *Live Your Dreams*, Scholastic, 2002
Sheppard, B. *Ian Thorpe*, Heinemann Library, 2002

NANCY WAKE
FitzSimons, P. *Nancy Wake: a biography of our greatest war heroine*, HarperCollins, 2001

SHANE WARNE
Pollard, J. *The Shane Warne Factor*, The Book Company, 1995

KARRIE WEBB
Tresidder, P. *Karrie Webb: the making of golf's tigress*, Pan Macmillan, 2000

JUDITH WRIGHT
Brady, V. *South of My Days: a biography of Judith Wright*, Angus & Robertson, 1998

NAT YOUNG
Young, N. *Nat's Nat and That's That: an autobiography*, Nymboida Press, 1998

Index

About the Author

Meredith Costain works full-time as a writer and editor. Her work ranges from picture books through to popular fiction and non-fiction for older readers. She is also the literary editor and a contributing writer for three children's magazines: *Comet*, *Explore* and *Challenge*. Meredith's books include *Freeing Billy*, *Oliver's Egg* and *Musical Harriet*, which was adapted for television by the ABC. She regularly presents writing workshops for kids and adults in libraries and schools.

Visit Meredith at: www.plasticine.com/mcostain